Solitude and Splendor

Living in the Schoolhouse

Maria Termini

Walk in Wonder,
maria termini
July 2007

PublishAmerica
Baltimore

ISBN: 1-4241-6928-3
PUBLISHED BY PUBLISHAMERICA, LLLP
www.publishamerica.com
Baltimore

Printed in the United States of America

Table of Contents

Introduction
To Follow My Dreams

With imagination, passion, hard work and luck, I was able to live my dream of living alone in a beautiful forest of countless trees. For many years before, I had hiked parts of the Appalachian Trail in Maine and New Hampshire. As I wandered through these vast forests, I would imagine living near the trail with only wild creatures for company. It would be so peaceful to live deep in a remote place where nothing could intrude from the chaotic modern world. I always dreamed of someday stepping back in time and doing just that and I held on to that dream of escape and adventure. When the chance came to live in the schoolhouse, I took it because this clearly seemed the way to make my dreams come true. My experience of living through the seasons in an old wooden schoolhouse in the White Mountain National Forest in western Maine is woven into the rich tapestry of my life. I deeply cherish that time of quiet solitude, the richness of the gifts of nature's splendor and the excitement of overcoming many challenges and fears. This schoolhouse became home, hearth, haven and art studio as I was able to go back to a slower time and to savor all the beauty around me.

As long as I can remember, I have always yearned to live in the green wild space of a forest. I consider trees as mysterious spirits in the way they touch the heavens and are still rooted in the earth. They are shelter to birds high above in their branches and to worms as well deep in their roots. Trees have inspired my art and there have even been times when I think of myself as a tree with my head in the clouds, feet on the ground and arms like branches reaching out to touch all the life I can. Even as a child living in a suburb of Washington, D.C., I sought the company of trees. I always preferred being outdoors. I have pleasant memories of following creeks where they flowed, catching frogs and salamanders, climbing trees to look for birds' nests and pretend I was a squirrel, blowing dandelion seeds into the wind and smelling all the flowers.

When I moved to the schoolhouse, I was ready to move from the town I lived in next to the busy urban area of Boston. My twin sons were grown to adulthood and had been living on their own for a while. They worked in the music business and were often on the road touring with rock or heavy metal bands. They did not need me on a daily basis and I was free of the intense responsibilities of being a mother. I was now able to explore other options in my life and, in particular, my deep desire to live in a forest. I was painting and exhibiting my art works in the Boston area as much as I could and also working as a substitute in the Boston Public Schools to earn money. I had not owned a television in many years but I was still deeply aware of the troubled state of the world, which weighed heavily upon me. The war in the Middle East and the burning of the oil wells in Iraq was a horror beyond comprehension. A recent gang shooting in a neighborhood park really scared me. I could hear the shots from my kitchen and they were too close for comfort. I was beginning to feel more and more overwhelmed by the crowded streets, pollution, trash, sirens, crime and grime. I longed to be in a quiet place near trees, deer, more birds, trails and ponds. I wanted to be able to paint and draw without interruptions. I clearly wanted to escape, but also to advance to an environment where my spirit could feel nourished with beauty and peace. I knew that place was a forest.

SOLITUDE AND SPLENDOR
LIVING IN THE SCHOOLHOUSE

I had rather impulsively bought an old somewhat abandoned schoolhouse located on an unplowed dirt road in western Maine surrounded by the White Mountain National Forest. For two years, I lived simply and well in that schoolhouse, deep in the forest embraced in the arms of countless trees. I had none of the common conveniences of modern life such as electricity, phones, television, electrical appliances and indoor plumbing. I was able to leave far behind many stressful distractions such as rush hour traffic, the rat race of commuting to a job, the hectic pace of city living, an overcrowded appointment book that made me measure each minute, and a compulsion to go everywhere and do too much. I was able to be receptive to the amazing wonder and beauty of nature, which has inspired my art and photographs and deep gratitude for this everyday blessing.

There were a lot of reasons for moving to this forest. My whole life seemed to be pointing me this way. I wanted to experience daily all the adventure and pleasure I felt when I hiked the Appalachian Trail. This is a well-known and well-trodden narrow path about 2,000 miles in length and accessible by foot only. It connects Springer Mountain in Georgia to Mt. Katahdin in Maine as it passes through the mountain ranges along the east coast of the United States. These include the Smokies, the Appalachians and, in New Hampshire, the White Mountains. On the trail, often it is possible to walk for days and not see a car nor come to a road. Some people hike the whole trail which usually takes three months in good summer weather. I was happy to do certain parts of it over and over again. I loved its wild tranquility. I breathed deeply the clean mountain air that often had the delightful scent of balsam pine. I would snack on the tasty tiny blueberries and cranberries at the summits. My fingers felt the varied textures of mossy rocks and bark, and delicate wildflowers were admired as individual works of art as I had often admired sculpture and paintings in a museum. The Appalachian Trail clearly had me under its spell.

It was in the early eighties that I had begun to hike the trail in earnest. It came about in a funny way that was a gift of coincidence.

I wasn't really intending to become fanatical about hiking, but it happened that both of my sons were in an Outward Bound camping experience that was starting from Newry, Maine, which was near the Appalachian Trail. For the first time since my twins were born, I would have ten days to myself without the daily responsibility of taking care of them. After I dropped my teenagers off at the Outward Bound base camp, I was so impressed by the sight of all these mountains and the wilderness that I decided I would go hiking in them myself. I was lucky because I had the time and freedom to do that.

So I got a pack, sleeping bag, trail map and a supply of nonperishable food like cheese, crackers, raisins and chocolate and began walking the Mahoosuc Trail, an approximately thirty mile section of the Appalachian Trail located between Route 2 and Route 26 on the border between Maine and New Hampshire. I spent eight days hiking the steep paths and slept mainly in the three-sided shelters, which are conveniently located about ten miles apart on the trail. My guide book said that this was considered to be one of the roughest parts of the Appalachian Trail, but I didn't care because there were so many mountains, brilliant stars and even the Northern Lights that glowed like a star sapphire. I didn't see a car for the whole trip. I loved finally reaching a summit after a long uphill struggle. I would feel as if I were on top of the world as I was rewarded with views of an endless sea of blue mountains in all directions. Because the Mahoosuc Trail was so difficult, there were few people on this part of the trail and I liked the solitude. I could tune into all the subtle sounds of the wind, chirping frogs, bird songs and the noisy dancing of chipmunks on dry leaves.

I found the Mahoosuc Trail was so outstandingly beautiful that I became hooked on hiking and continued to come back to this trail many times through the years. I needed very little to survive and could carry everything on my back. There was always plenty of cool, clean drinking water from the many brooks. I knew there were deer, moose and bears all around me even though they tended to hear me coming and keep out of sight. I saw lots of their droppings and prints in muddy places. There were even a few placid ponds hidden in the thick patches of evergreens where they shimmered with ground fog and gentle ripples. My favorite pond was Gentian Pond, which had its own shelter where I often slept. As the day ended, I would stare at the pond and be hypnotized by the endless ripples that flowed from its center towards patches of pink and white water lilies. This was a great place to swim and catch the sun on the warm rocks on its sandy shore and watch the dragonflies take off. I was often completely alone here as other hikers were in more of a hurry to move on. One August morning, I had some good company as a moose and her calf joined me.

The biggest challenge for my knees was the famous and much dreaded Mahoosuc Notch. Its reputation for extreme difficulty preceded it as the topic of conversation in nearby shelters. The Notch was a mile-long stretch of huge boulders the size of small trucks. At every step I had to decide whether to go over, under or around these massive obstacles. I felt like my body was a chess piece and I had to carefully determine the right move in order not to fall into an abyss. Sheer rock rose high on both sides of the notch to dramatic heights and the only way out was to keep going through the notch. Deep in the rocks below my feet, I could see permanent lingering patches of ice and snow that persisted even in July. Hiking the Mahoosuc Trail was exhausting but exhilarating. The trail soon became a magnet for my body and soul. I was very slow and took my time and hiked alone so I could nap whenever I wanted. Peace of body and spirit always came through the struggle. After a hiking trip, I always returned to the city and my creative work feeling refreshed and renewed. It got to be that I wanted to spend as much time as I could hiking.

I have become aware that so much of my life has led me to closer contact with nature. My life has been blessed to be full of adventures in beautiful places that I could never have planned, but did have the power to imagine. Despite economic challenges and often the outright poverty of being a single mother, I have enjoyed raising my children and doing a lot of other interesting things such as creating artworks, traveling with my twins in Europe for a year, driving solo in a bus to Central America, fixing up houses in Hawaii and the Virgin Islands, working with Habitat for Humanity in Nicaragua and Boston, working with refugees in Texas, serving in the U.S. Peace Corps in Bolivia and much more. I have been persistent and passionate about creating art but I also wanted and needed to do a lot of other things. In many ways I think my art draws from a deep well of personal experiences and art and life are never separate for me. I enjoy doing a lot of different things and often think of my life as a mixed media work of art in progress using rich color, texture, images, excitement, a search for justice, reverence for the earth, music and so much more.

My life I did not follow anyone else's plan. I have had an exciting life but it was hard work and required being open to possibilities. I left home as soon as I could, which was at the age of eighteen. I felt like I broke out of the expected pattern of life for a daughter in an Italian-American family in the fifties. I was the oldest girl and had six brothers. My father had rigid views that seemed to present to me only the possibility of a narrow and boring life mired in domesticity. As a woman, my obvious and accepted destiny was to have been to get married, have many children, and obey my husband. While I will always be grateful to my father for sending me to an academically rigorous all-girls Catholic high school, I never once sensed any encouragement from him for me go to college. I did know that money was very tight in my family then, but it might have been possible. Many years later, I heard from one of my brothers that my parents felt there would be no point in higher education for me if I was only going to be a wife and mother, which was the only role for them to imagine me in.

I rebelled and saw my own future through a much wider lens. I was greatly aware of how tired my mother always seemed from child bearing, child rearing, cooking and never-ending housework. In a few instances, I do recall her joyously singing and holding a cute toddler but generally I saw that she was exhausted, prone to illnesses and worn down from the stress and strain of so much work in the home. More than once she said, perhaps facetiously, that she wished she had chosen the calmer life of a nun. Our small house, stretching at the seams with seven children underfoot, was always noisy and chaotic. There always was a line at the bathroom. I longed for peace and quiet in which to read and paint but a room of my own or any kind of solitude here was an impossibility.

In my family, in the 1950s, there was a rigid division of labor. All the household work was women's work. But there were few women here—only my mother and myself. We were responsible for all the cooking, cleaning, washing, ironing, mending and more. Men worked outside the home. It often seemed that in my lopsided family, my six younger brothers were completely exempt from doing any housework because they were male. This seemed unfair and made me very mad. I know that housework is simply work and should be shared fairly, but when I was a child, my father, especially, held to the belief that women had the fixed role of only working in the house and in our house there was plenty of work. He did not have a vision of another way. I knew that I did not want to have a life like my mother's. I knew that I had to be free. I had visions of traveling and creating colorful paintings. I had an enormous imagination that helped me keep my dreams alive. It was enhanced by reading many adventure books and *National Geographic Magazines* and a sense of the fascinating wide world absorbed from collecting postage stamps. I left home as soon as I could. I felt very free even though I worked full-time to put myself through college and graduate school at Catholic University in Washington, D.C. I did this to follow my dream of being an artist. When I graduated I was proud to be the first in my family to get a degree. I clearly remember that my mother said that she was proud of me for the hard work I had done. My father said nothing and his silence was painful to me.

My life embarked onto often unfamiliar territory as I did not really know other women like myself. I looked for women I admired in the public sphere. My role models could easily include the diverse trio of Mother Teresa, Jacqueline Kennedy, and Tina Turner for their compassionate charity, graceful elegance and musical energy respectively. After I received my master's degree, I was blessed to become the mother of twins. Raising twins without the support of a husband and still being an artist required a lot of expert juggling of tasks. I quickly learned the value of organizing my time as I also had various teaching jobs to earn much-needed cash. I always managed to have a room to use as a studio and worked as much as possible to create colorful silkscreen prints, collages, drawings and painting. Often I painted deep into the night as my children slept and I had, at last, quiet and uninterrupted time.

Through the years, I developed skills for living in the city and coping with adversity, which worked well for living in the schoolhouse. It was never easy to sell my art which I was inspired to create. I did not earn much money as an artist, but I knew I had to be an artist. To keep body and soul together for me and my children, I learned to live on very little, to find furniture, clothes and other useful things in the trash, to fix things, and to do repairs on my house. Not having a lot of money led me to develop these skills. I was very happy to have a home of my own when I was able to buy a wreck of a house for a ridiculously very low price. My house needed a lot of work and I could not afford to hire people to fix it. I discovered that I had a talent for carpentry although a lot of my early work was trial and error. Working with wood felt natural and a hammer felt like an extension of my hand. I could bang nails with great confidence. I scrounged free wood from construction sites around my neighborhood to build furniture and built-ins. I loved sawdust in my hair and breathing the fragrance of fresh cut wood as I did carpentry.

The long years of raising twins seem like a spinning blur. In addition to keeping us fed, clothed and sheltered, I had become good at fulfilling the travel impulse that let me experience so much of the beauty of the world. In 1971, after I could free myself from a destructive relationship, work a lot and save some money, I flew to Europe with my then-six-year-old twin sons. We lived for a year in a small Italian village called Vicovaro that appeared to have been untouched since medieval times. I was thirty then and it was the first time in my life I had seen mountains and I was amazed by their size and the way the light would change their colors during the day. I spent many hours walking though this enchanted environment and painting everything that snagged my spirit including the clouds and donkeys. I felt close to the earth in the Italian countryside and was very aware of the seasons of planting, harvesting grapes, and picking olives. My Italian ancestors had been farmers in Italy and a strong connection to the land is in my blood and spirit.

In that same year, my sons and I also covered a lot of miles to other countries in Europe, drove to Morocco and sailed to Israel from Greece. I saw places that astounded me including smoking volcanos, the salt-filled Dead Sea, fields of endless grain and smiling sunflowers, snow-covered mountains and soft sandy beaches in Crete. Back in the Boston area, I continually sought out the parks and forests near me to satisfy my need for trees and open spaces. A sailing trip with a friend among uninhabited islands off the Maine coast convinced me that I could survive and thrive in wild places. All this was inspiration for my art and led me to develop a deep awareness of the beauty of the landscape.

After my sons grew up, my love for nature grew stronger from intense traveling to countries in Central America. In 1986, I spent a year in my rusty but stubborn 1972 VW bus driving slowly alone through Mexico, Guatemala, Honduras and Nicaragua. I learned Spanish on the way and camped out in secluded places in the mountains with amazing views. I saw these countries in a deep way that tourists on guided tours could not. Images of extreme poverty, dramatic vistas from mountain tops, and destruction of the environment are etched in my memory forever. Once while driving on a breathtakingly beautiful mountain road in Chiapas, Mexico, I pulled over to a spot indicated by a sign that said: "Scenic Vista." I sadly saw that it was being used as a dump site and was cluttered with literally tons of garbage and empty plastic bottles. I saw close up how this earth is threatened as people struggle to survive and there is just no place for trash to go and there is just too much of it.

Five months of that year long road trip were spent in a very remote jungle area of Nicaragua near the Honduran border that abounded with tropical animals like parrots and iguanas. I parked my bus in a small meadow and camped there. My bus was very good housing compared to the straw and twig huts most of my neighbors lived in. I worked at a Habitat for Humanity project with very poor families. I enjoyed getting to know many Nicaraguans who were very friendly and gracious. It felt good to be able to help build sturdy houses with concrete floors and tiled roofs that made for healthier living conditions. I shared and improved my carpentry skills a lot. I fortunately had all my tools with me in my bus. I learned and appreciated so much of the diversity of the natural world as I explored the jungle around me. I admired the white-flowered *pitaya* cactus and the round fruit of the *jicaro* tree that grew right off the branches. In Nicaragua I lived very close to the earth, and through the wraparound windows of my bus, I could always see the brilliant stars above the silhouettes of the palm trees before I fell asleep.

Another amazing unplanned opportunity to deepen my knowledge and wonder of flowers and plants materialized a few years after I returned to the Boston area. A friend sent me to his parents' home in Hawaii for three months to do a lot of repairs. I stayed in that paradise for three months and was amazed at the exuberance of the plants and flowers. Bright red ginger and the wing-like bird of paradise flowers seemed to just grow like wildflowers in the rich volcanic soil. I saw monster fiddle head ferns four feet tall and many varieties of palm trees. I lived next to a greenhouse filled with over a thousand varieties of orchids each with its own very unique fragrance ranging from that of exquisite perfume to a repulsive detergent. At night I would take individual potted orchids into my room and draw them as I was endlessly intrigued by their extravagant combinations of petals and patterns. On my days off, I hiked into the mountains or dragged my feet in the smooth sand of the beaches filling my spirit with more and more of the beauty of the earth.

All these experiences clearly led me to dream of a forest home. The schoolhouse showed up at the right time in my life as I felt called to live deeply immersed in the forest. Somehow things fell in place for this move. For the last couple of years I had taken out a subscription to the local newspaper in Bethel, Maine. From my urban home, I became aware of the unique flavor of life in a small town where most people were related to each other and had ancestral roots that went back centuries to when the area was first settled. Each week as I read the *Bethel Citizen*, I was participating vicariously in the life of this small town. Out of curiosity, I would read the real estate ads. When I saw an ad for the schoolhouse, which included eighteen acres of forest, something clicked in my brain and I knew right away that I wanted to buy it. I called the real estate broker's office and I was told that the property had no electricity, heat, access to phone lines and running water. The road was described as "seasonal." On the phone, the broker clearly explained to me that this meant the road was not plowed in the winter and was, therefore, not accessible by car for about five months of the year. This would mean walking a mile each way to go back and forth between my car and the schoolhouse. I knew this would be inconvenient but I had strong legs. Right away I drove up to Maine, saw the schoolhouse and fell in love with it in its dilapidated state and completely ignored its faults. It was love at first sight and I didn't even wait to sleep on this purchase. I wrote out a check for a deposit even though I knew well the adage "love is blind." I still wanted to buy that schoolhouse despite no utilities and no plowing in the winter.

Life in the schoolhouse would surely be very different in many ways. I did not have all the answers or even all the questions. I did have a confident feeling about living in the schoolhouse. My life experiences compelled me to move to this wilderness where not even a power line disturbed it. I wanted the new challenge of living here. After living with siblings, children or lovers for so much of my life, I craved solitude: creative solitude in which to paint and just plain solitude in which to do nothing. This abounded in the schoolhouse, and more so when the road was blocked with snow for long months. Yet, I was always aware that the flip side of luxurious solitude was painful loneliness. In the schoolhouse, I couldn't just pick up the phone to call a friend and my car would be a mile away through thick snow. Surviving loneliness would not be easy. Moving to another state would be like starting over and I wondered how easily I could make new friends.

Unanswered questions swirled around my mind like a whirlpool as I prepared for the big move. Would it be enough to just be an artist here and lose myself in the creative process with no hope of sharing my work with anyone? Could I survive economically here? Was there any paid work around here that would use my skills? Would I become some eccentric recluse, forget to bathe, and talk outrageously to imaginary people? I doubted that since I am actually very sociable. Would I eat strange mushrooms, get sick and die and not be found until after mud season, if at all? Would I fail to keep the stove burning and freeze to death when it was twenty degrees below zero? What if I ran out of matches to light the stove? What if a bear attacked me as I bushwacked alone in the thick forest?

I was very curious about these questions and myself. I knew that the answers lay only in the actual experience of living in the schoolhouse. The schoolhouse had been neglected for many years and obviously needed a lot of work, care and love. It was definitely a handyperson's special and well suited for a compulsive fixer-upper like myself. I had carpentry and construction skills and physical energy to do hard work and make my dream happen. As I lived in the schoolhouse, I hoped to appreciate that balance of physical work and doing art and being and not doing. I hoped to eliminate the noise and static of modern life and to fully experience all this wonder and the marvelous rhythm of the seasons.

I eagerly prepared for this new adventure and made plans to sell my house in Massachusetts. I sorted through my possessions making decisions about what things I needed to have in the schoolhouse. Of course, nothing electrical would have been useful. My houseplants would not survive in the schoolhouse and I gave them away. I would bring all my paints, pencils, pastels, paper, brushes and canvass. I found places to store all the art work I had created in the last twenty years and began to pack. I had to sell my piano, a huge Mason Hamlin upright that had wonderful tone which I had played for years. I immediately missed its presence but it would not have stayed healthy in the cold and damp of the schoolhouse. I was going to have to be content with my classical guitar. On December seventh, I had a huge birthday party and said goodbye to old friends and invited them to visit. They did not seem very enthusiastic when I explained about the lack of running water and the outhouse which were minor details to me. All I could think about was having this vast forest of eighteen acres which would be my home and how I would live my dream.

Chapter 1
Moving In

A bitter cold persisted stubbornly into the heart of February but it did not chill the excitement I felt as, at last, I began to move into my new-old schoolhouse. I was free from a daily job because I had just quit working in the Boston Public Schools as an all-subjects substitute teacher on the high school level. This job had its hectic and trying moments as the students would often kick back and misbehave with vigor because they thought most substitute teachers were not able to follow through on their bad behavior. Now I did not have to go to work in the morning anymore at six and I would soon be out of the turmoil of the city and sheltered in the serenity of the forest in winter. I did not care how cold it was up there since I was ready to live my dream.

In the early morning brilliant sunshine, I drove my Honda Civic hatchback north from Boston on the interstate to Maine. At exit eleven, I curved through the small town of Gray with its old brick buildings next to a McDonald's. Then for about an hour and a half, I stayed on Route 26 which was an endless busy two lane road that took me past small towns like Poland Springs, Oxford, and Norway separated by the frozen fields of small farms. As the roads became narrower, I felt like I was in a time tunnel being transported backwards to a quieter era. After I reached Norway, the tall peak of Mount Washington from the Presidential Range in New Hampshire greeted me and its ice and snow covered summit reflected the sun's rays like a lighthouse.

Tonight I would spend my first night sleeping in the schoolhouse which I had recently bought. I had already stuffed my backpack with food, candles, essential things, and my sleeping bag. I had even checked to make sure that I remembered matches. I drove to the end of Flat Road which was very icy and arrived at the last possible place to park in the early afternoon. This was where the school bus turned around and the end of the plowed part of the road. I was relieved to find that there was enough space to park my small car in front of a snow bank where it would still be off the road and not get gobbled up by a monster snow plow.

It was important to get to the schoolhouse as soon as possible. Winter days are very short and I needed to take advantage of as much of the day's light as I could. I quickly swung my heavy pack onto my back and climbed over the small mountain of snow left by the plow. On the other side, I entered a totally white and quiet world as I began the mile-long walk on Flat Road which soon changed its name to: USFS 7 with a small metal sign and I knew this meant: "United States Forest Service Road Number 7." The road was totally blocked with snow. Of course, I knew this would be true. It was Maine and February. This was exactly what the real estate broker had told me, or maybe warned me about. No vehicle could get through this deep unplowed snow until late April in mud season. The road was drivable only when there was no snow clogging it. With one foot in front of the other and aware of the sound of my boots crunching the snow and dazzled by the whiteness of all the snow, I began the walk for the first of many times to my new home in the forest.

Uninterrupted winter stillness lay under a smooth blue sky. I was totally alone and aware of the rustling of the transparent dried leaves still hanging on the low beech trees. I was going to an adventure of wonder deep in the forest. I knew there was no heat in the schoolhouse, but details like this were not going to bother me. I had a sleeping bag and a sense of mission that obliterated any fear. I was able to avoid walking in deep snow by keeping to the narrow tracks made by cross country skiers. After about a half hour, the white schoolhouse which was the only building on this road came into view. Snow had drifted to a height of three feet against the front door. I kicked it with my boots to get access. I had five keys to the three front doors which finally got me into the big open main space which was the one room schoolhouse's only classroom. Right away I noticed how the air smelled old as I entered a huge, dank and dusty cave that was the one and only classroom. The frayed green shades were pulled down over all the windows. I immediately pulled them up only to find that effort almost useless because all the windows except one were boarded up on the outside. It was already getting darker and I knew that night would be here very soon.

The sound of my heavy boots echoed in the silent space. I quickly walked around and checked out as much as I could. The attached outhouse was creepy looking but would surely be usable. There were bodies of dead mice and other larger unidentifiable rodents everywhere and I tried to avoid stepping on them. An old white enameled Glenwood cooking stove hovered in one corner. It looked sort of stupid there because there was no way that it could serve to heat this place because it was not connected to the chimney. There was no firewood anywhere in sight. I knew I needed to get a wood stove as soon as I could for heat. However, I was resigned to the reality that it could not be delivered until the snow would melt and the road would again be passable for vehicles.

My old schoolhouse had been built around 1850 and was an active learning institution for about seventy-five years in which grades one through eight were all taught in the same big room and by one teacher. Now this space was filled with bunk beds, junk and old furniture most of which was broken beyond repair. There were some interesting things: an old calendar from the forties with a picture of a moose drinking in a lake at a colorful sunset, *Life* magazines from the fifties, and dried food products like powdered mustard and baking powder in rusted tins. It was kind of a small archeological site, but I wasn't going to preserve it since it was just too filthy.

While I still had energy and daylight, I unrolled my sleeping bag on an old double bed with a mattress covered with mouse droppings. Then I found some old blankets in a corner and layered them on top of my sleeping bag. Somehow an old pillow stuffed with escaping feathers materialized and the smell was tolerable. So I added that to my sleeping arrangement. I started lighting candles and looked around the cavernous darkness and began to think of all the things I would need to do here to make this place habitable. My first priority would be major cleaning. Tomorrow I would go to town and get a broom, trash bags and a dustpan. Then, I thought about how I could make the windows bigger to get more light so I can enjoy the views of the forest surrounding me. Soon, I would build a deck off the side door. Next, I would get used to the outhouse, get a wood stove, get firewood, figure out how to use a wood stove, plant a garden, and more and more. This place was like a blank canvass full of potential and waiting for creative touches from my imagination which was even now in overdrive.

Stomach growling signaled the dinner time. From my pack I produced a light supper of salty corn chips, chocolate and orange juice. One of the crumbling *Life* magazines tempted me into reading it by candlelight with its black and white pictures of a young Frank Sinatra crooning his songs to fans before the era of television. Around six o'clock, I crawled into my sleeping bag wearing everything I had. It was so cold that there was really nothing else I could do but sleep.

I got more sleep than I usually did and I had a lot of dreams that went on and on in an unconnected manner. Nothing intruded on the total quiet all around me and my slumbering subconscious rambled unimpeded. I did keep waking up through the night with cold toes. The musty smell of the room that had been closed for many years pressed around me but I quickly went back to sleep. As I awoke after dawn, the total quiet was spread all around me. I had never been in such a quiet place. The silence was new to me and like a piece of strange fruit. I was so used to the constant noises of the urban area where I had lived for so many years in a small house wedged between the trolley tracks and a busy divided highway. I kept expecting to hear the sounds of cars and trucks. During my first night in the schoolhouse, I felt safe despite the cold, surrounded by the forest, itself asleep under its deep blanket of snow.

Handyperson's Special of a Schoolhouse

Slowly the dark winter morning moved to the certainty of daylight and I knew it was safe to leave the warm comfort of my sleeping bag and blankets. My every breath produced a cloud of steam in the arctic schoolhouse interior which was like a walk-in freezer. I quickly shed the layers of blankets and began an energetic imitation of tap dancing on the hard rock maple floor and moving continuously to keep as warm as possible. I had a beautiful jog back to my car and shot straight down Flat Road to the corner with Route 2 and the Mountain View Restaurant. I embraced the warmth there and delightedly consumed a hearty logger's breakfast of greasy sausages, eggs over easy and thick toast from homemade bread with maple syrup and all the steaming coffee I could pour into myself. In town, I bought more food, cleaning supplies and trash bags and soon, again with a full pack, I returned to the schoolhouse using my brand new broom as a walking stick. Once inside, I started sweeping and picking up large quantities of trash. I was keeping warm by working so furiously that I was almost sweating and the cold wasn't a problem as long as I stayed in motion.

I needed more light and air and the side door in the big room refused to open. It had been secured to the frame with locks and large nails. There was an inner and outer door—both of which had padlocks for which I did not have the keys. Luckily, I had packed in the right tools. Sawing off the padlocks with a hacksaw was the easy part. The outer solid wood door was toe-nailed shut at an inaccessible angle, and there was no way I could have opened it with just my wrecking bar. I had to wedge the saw blade between the door and the threshold and saw off about ten thick nails. It was hard work that took about three hours and the continual pushing of the blade against the nails cramped my fingers. Each time I sawed through one big three penny nail there would be another one hidden away. I lusted for electricity and a power saw which would have let me do the job in five minutes. I was mad at the fanaticism of the former owner for being so worried about security and going overboard on nailing that side door shut. It seemed like he wanted it shut for all eternity and never thought to realize that someone like me would want to open it. I figured he mainly used the schoolhouse as a camp when he hunted and the view meant nothing to him. No normal person could have ever opened that heavy door. Nail by nail, I made slow but steady progress. At last I was victorious after I sawed through the last nail and was able to swing open the door. I was rewarded with an exquisite view of the beginning sunset, the nearby brook and the forest. Now there was more light in here and, of course, more cold.

By now, I had packed in some oil lamps which, when lit, cast a warm soft glow about the inside of the schoolhouse. On this second night, as I again lay on the filthy bed stuffed into my sleeping bag, I heard only the sounds of my own breathing and the gentle wind softly whistling around the tops of the pine trees.

I again slept well despite waking up now and then as the wind changed into a fierce angry prowling tiger. To my surprise and delight, the schoolhouse stood firm with neither creaking nor shaking. I was warm as I slept even though the new thermometer I had bought declared that it was fifteen degrees inside the schoolhouse. It was probably the same outside. I had never been in this kind of cold overnight except for sleeping in my car when traveling, but I was dry and OK and my body heat filled the sleeping bag. In the morning, my orange juice was naturally frozen rock hard and I tried to thaw it over an oil lamp. I gave up and pretended it was a popsicle. I was ready to go to town again and do some more shopping. I somehow managed to measure the windows even though my fingers were turning to ice cubes and I could hardly hold the pencil to write the measurements. I wanted to come back with curtains that would fit into the space and make it beautiful as soon as possible.

I got moving and scurried up the road to my warm car before frostbite really set in and while I could still think. It was colder outside and the snappy wind bit my face as I walked as fast as I could since my toes were beginning to feel frozen. When I got to the car, the key would not go into the lock and the doors were frozen shut. So I managed to open the hatch back window and crawl in. My car sprung to life like a startled cat and in just a few minutes I was again soaking in what seemed like tropical warmth at the Mountain View Restaurant and thawing my feet out on their heating grate and my insides with hot coffee. This became a necessary habit.

I drove the long way into Bethel on Grover Hill Road and drove on a ridge that gave me great views of the shiny snow-covered fields and dormant apple orchards with soft mountains rising up in the distance. I walked around the town of Bethel and saw to my delight that there was a small skating rink on the town common. Browsing in the hardware store on Maine Street was a fascinating learning experience. I saw all kinds of things that were appropriate for a rural area including chicken feed, hardware cloth, delicate fishing lures and bright orange and camouflage hunting attire. I took a serious look at electrical generators. I thought it might be useful to have one just for occasional use with power tools. I had been told that getting a utility line to the schoolhouse would be prohibitively expensive since the nearest pole was a mile away. I also started looking longingly at wood stoves and wondered if I could learn to use one correctly without causing a fire. Meanwhile, I got only what I could carry in which included a very essential small two burner propane stove and a canister of gas that could fit in my backpack.

On my third day in the schoolhouse, I set up the small stove and life really improved. I was able to get water from the nearby brook that never froze which I boiled in a tea kettle with a green wood handle rescued from a pile of trash. Soon my cold hands caressed a hot cup of instant coffee that never smelled so rich especially in the dull air of the schoolhouse. Now, I could cook and even heat water to wash my face. But, it was too cold to even think of washing the rest of me.

That afternoon, there were intermittent snow showers and bits of glorious sunshine. While I had daylight, I continued to furiously hack away at the endless cleaning and the big classroom began to look less like a cave and more like a human dwelling. I gritted my teeth and swept up a lot of the dead mice and larger critters which I think were chipmunks. Some of them I had to scrape off the floor with a putty knife. Luckily all the bodies were frozen solid and did not smell. It was a lot cleaner now and I did not have to be so careful where I stepped.

After a while, I was surprised to the hear the sound of human voices and I saw two men on snowshoes standing outside my front door. They said that they had seen the door I had left open for more sunlight and were concerned that someone might have broken into the schoolhouse. I introduced myself as the new owner. They said they were foresters out looking at trees professionally. If they thought I was crazy for being here in the dead of winter with no heat, they had the grace not to mention it for which I was grateful. After they left, I walked to Crocker Pond as the day ended. I returned to the schoolhouse in the silent descending darkness as the moon came out giving me all the soft blue light I needed to see perfectly. I rejoiced that I could now begin to live my dream in this forest-filled peaceful snowy tranquility.

Chapter 2
Mud City and Its Schoolhouse

It was a new experience to live in the schoolhouse all the time. I could no longer escape to the creature comfort of my previous home in Brookline with heat at the turn of the thermostat and always the option of a tub of hot water with the turn of a faucet. Bubble bath was useless as I had neither a tub nor running water. Of course, being closer to the North Pole, it was colder and with a lot more snow. Spring and summer came later than they did in Massachusetts which I soon came to regard as balmy and tropical. I quickly learned that Maine has its own extra season: that special season of spring thaw and squishiness called "mud season" in April and most of May when mud is everywhere and unavoidable. The area around my schoolhouse had been known as Mud City. I imagined that someone was feeling humorous in mud season and felt moved to name his neighborhood after the abundance of mud. Or they might have observed some of the many moose in the area as they wallowed and danced in the muddy boggy areas.

In the middle of the nineteenth century, Mud City had been a thriving agricultural community. There were enough families with young children living here to need their own one-room schoolhouse. The dirt road right in front of the schoolhouse was at that time part of a main intersection with Cod Fish Ledge Road. Inside the schoolhouse, it often seemed that the walls could talk and it was not hard to imagine the young voices of the students filling the air of their one-room classroom as they recited their lessons in unison and their scattered laughter as they played outside. Through my friend, Peter Lenz, who was most knowledgeable about local history, I met an older woman in nearby Norway (Maine) who told me that she remembered attending this schoolhouse in the nineteen twenties. She and her classmates would climb around the ledge during school recess as if it were a jungle gym.

Settling Mud City was undoubtedly heavy and hard work as it was a very rocky area. Much intense labor was needed for cutting trees, clearing the fields, stone by stone, to plant crops and apple trees and create grazing land. This was all done before the invention of electricity and mechanized farm equipment using human labor and that of horses and oxen. The clearing of the fields led to the building of the stone walls to fence in meadows. I saw these walls often as I walked in the forest.

Surviving here must have become more and more difficult, possibly as the result of droughts that hindered agricultural efforts. The area of Mud City became abandoned as people eventually migrated to more prosperous urban areas with commerce and factories in the nineteen thirties. There came a point where there were no longer sufficient numbers of school-age children to study and learn at the schoolhouse and it was sold to a local farmer, Mr. Jim Everett. The old schoolhouse became a camp for hunters to use. When I moved in, it appeared to have been unused for many years and the interior was coated with the thick dust of time.

As I started looking at the land around the schoolhouse more seriously, I discovered the ghosts of the old apple trees that had been planted in an orchard almost a hundred years ago. The ancient trees had been planted in straight lines and at precise intervals. Their old knurled trunks twisted up to the sky and sucker shoots grew even now at the base of the trunks over a hundred years later. Sometimes I even saw an occasional apple on the traces of these trees. It was there because it was too high for the deer to reach it.

I was delighted with the babbling brook ran through my land and was the main source of my water where it passed near the schoolhouse. An old timer told me that once it was possible to fish for trout in the brook. This might be why the granite ledge in front of the schoolhouse was, perhaps sarcastically, called Codfish Ledge. Maybe they thought they were catching cod which is an ocean fish. Most likely they caught brook trout which I never saw.

My schoolhouse itself was a simple rectangular shape with a peaked roof on a post and beam frame of rot-proof cedar logs. It was about a hundred and fifty years old and wrapped in its original wooden clapboard that needed paint. The floor was rock maple, a wood of fierce hardness. Amazingly there was no wood rot in the building itself because it sat high on a stone foundation that kept it dry. The roof was of corrugated metal that resounded noisily with rain drops like a stampede of squirrels. The outhouse was connected by a short hallway to the schoolhouse and was raised up about four feet off the ground.

As the snow melted in spring, I began to see that the schoolhouse was surrounded by thick overgrowth. Slowly I began to clear away the tangled brush to keep water off of the foundation and low clapboards. I found to my great delight that fragrant wild rose and lilac bushes emerged and flowered in the first spring I was there. They must have been originally planted around 1920. I also had lots of day lilies in front of the windows that bloomed abundantly when freed of competing weeds. Miraculously humming birds appeared on the scene in summer. Their tiny iridescent green bellies shone in the sun as they hovered and buzzed into the lilies to sip nectar with their long bills. Mud City proved early on to be full of wonder and delight.

When I arrived at my schoolhouse, my cares and troubles seemed to float away and I felt like I was in a different and simpler time. This was a cure for my bad case of "future shock." There were no power lines, asphalt or other modern developments that intruded on the stillness here. I could easily imagine horses tied up at a hitching post, cows and sheep grazing peacefully in the verdant meadows bordered by stone walls, apples turning red and ripe in the orchard. I could even hear the soft sound of an apple falling to the ground in the fall on the dry leaves. I imagined cackling chickens underfoot scratching for grain. Here I was in a slower time and able to savor the beauty around me. The rat race of the city was light years away and I did not miss it.

The closest real town to me was Bethel. It was originally founded in 1774 and had the name of "Sudbury Canada" because the original settlers had arrived here from Sudbury, Massachusetts, as part of a campaign to conquer Canada. After the American Revolution, the town grew rapidly and its name was changed to Bethel, a Hebrew word from the Book of Genesis which means "House of God." This was most appropriate for such a beautiful area. There was even a street called Paradise Road that ascends to a ridge with houses that are resplendent with ethereal views of an eternity of mountains in all directions. During the previous ten years I spent hiking the Mahoosuc Trail, I often passed through the town of Bethel in western Maine so I was familiar with it.

On a topographical map, such as the trail maps that the Appalachian Mountain Club publishes, my schoolhouse was shown as a tiny black square smaller than a fly. It stands in a part of the White Mountain National Forest, located in the unorganized township of Albany in the very western part of Maine near the New Hampshire border. There were some vacation homes scattered about but mainly this area seemed to me like all dirt roads and thick forest richly embroidered with pine, spruce, fir, hemlock, birch, maple, oak and an occasional tamarack. In Albany, there was no visible government and no stores or offices which was fine with me. On the corner of an intersection, there did stand the white clapboard Albany Town Hall. It was mostly closed except when there was an election or a need to discuss a hot topic like a proposed gambling casino. Then the town hall would come alive for the occasion as concerned citizens gathered to be part of the democratic process. I went to some of these meetings and was pleased to see great turnouts and that people were very concerned about keeping the rural character of the area.

There were mountains all around this part of Maine. A few had been developed into downhill skiing areas. There were also innumerable cross country ski trails many of which were automatically created from logging roads and unplowed dirt roads. My land was bordered by three private owners and on the fourth side by a section of the White Mountain National Forest owned by the United States Government. I was surprised to find out that there were actually many areas of private land within the National Forest since I had formerly believed that it was all one big continuous area.

The nearest big river was the mighty Androscoggin. It was about five miles north of my schoolhouse. It flowed east out of Gorham, New Hampshire, to Maine, along Route 2, through Bethel, and then to Rumford where it thundered down giant falls and provided electrical power for the Boise-Cascade paper mill. After winter, the Androscoggin could grow in size and sound with the melting snow, spill its banks and greatly flood low-lying areas. It was calmer in the late summer and it was a great place to canoe and see close-up the habitats of water birds. The area had many opportunities for outdoor recreation. The Appalachian Trail, which included my favorite stretch, the Mahoosuc Trail, was about ten miles to my west. South of the Mahoosuc Mountains were the White Mountains in New Hampshire. Sometimes on clear days from high places I could see the snow-covered summit of Mt. Washington, the highest peak in the northeast of the United States and famous for its bad weather. The White Mountains are very popular with both day hikers as well as through hikers on the Appalachian Trail. There were also some nearby state parks. Now that I lived here, I did not have to go any great distance to enjoy all this.

After the intense traffic jams of the Boston area, Oxford County seemed tranquil and sufficiently far away from the busy Maine coast which attracted hordes of lobster-hungry tourists in the summer. Traffic gridlock was an unheard of concept. Bethel had no parking meters which was a welcome relief. Moose on the road were the major local traffic hazards. In mating season, moose would wander far from the forest, even down the streets of Bethel looking for a partner. Motor vehicle accidents with moose could be very serious for humans and beasts, especially since the moose were very large animals. Although there were many summer visitors to nearby natural attractions and campgrounds, things in Mud City stayed calm. There would be a few more vehicles going back and forth on my road to the Crocker Pond campsite and more summer visitors in the stores in Bethel, but there was never any sense of crowding because there was so much open space up here. There really was no rush hour at all.

Jobs in western Maine were different than those in the city where many people worked indoors in offices. I learned about logging which was a major source of income for a lot of people here. Pine and other soft woods produced pulp for the paper mills. Hardwoods like maple and oak were cut and dried for the different furniture making businesses. I learned about the huge tractors used for hauling logs out of the rough terrain of the forest called skidders. The loggers had their own culture that had to do with the fine points of chainsaws and their maintenance. Loggers were always outdoors and I was very curious about how they survived the thick bugs. I was told that used chainsaw oil was the best repellent. I tried it and it worked but was messy. People up here had different things to talk about. How and when you got your firewood in for the winter was a big conversation topic. People would start boasting in August that they had already gotten their entire supply of wood for their stove on their premises either by chopping and splitting it themselves or having it delivered.

Oxford County's original inhabitants were Native Americans from the Passamoquoddy tribe. Their descendants are still here. Later immigrants from what was probably the equally cold country of Finland settled in the area. The Finns brought their bathing customs with them and this explains why there are a lot of small wooden sauna houses in people's backyards. There was, for reasons I can't explain, a tendency for towns in Oxford County to be named after foreign places. It could have been a yearning for Europe. I doubt if there was anyone in Mexico, Maine, located outside of Rumford, who could speak more than three words of Spanish. I soon got to know places up here called Paris, South Paris, Norway, Poland, and Sweden. The names of places in Europe sure livened up the map.

I explored a lot but was also happy staying put as there was so much to see right around my schoolhouse. I loved to just wander aimlessly, follow stone walls, creeks and old logging roads, and explore ponds, fields of wildflowers, blackberry patches and marshes. I was excited when I finally found an old abandoned mica mine off the road to Crocker Pond and harvested some big glittering books of pages of this flakey shiny mineral that once was used as glass in stove doors and electrical fuses. Hidden deep in the mountains here in secret locations were other minerals, like tourmaline gemstones.

One of my favorite day hikes was to climb Albany Mountain. The trail began a half mile from my schoolhouse and crossed a brook a number of times. There was always clear cool drinking water in shady glades. The trail went straight up for about two thousand feet through wooded forest. There were lots of moose nearby because I often encountered their round droppings. After a few years, I noticed how part of the trail had to be rerouted after some beavers chewed down enough trees to build a dam on the brook that created a pond and covered the trail with several feet of water. There were many tree stumps around the pond that looked as if they had been sharpened in the giant pencil sharpener that was the mouth of a beaver. Albany Mountain has a huge summit of smooth granite with yellow and white lichens and Irish moss interspersed with stunted evergreens. The trail ends at a cliff with a sharp drop overlooking amazing views in all directions. In the late summer on the summit, the tiny cranberries and blueberries would ripen. They were a lot of work to pick but worth it because of their sweetness.

Little by little, I began to settle into my new home and neighborhood. It was quite a different environment from the city but it seemed like a natural transition to be here. I was told, as a kind of joke, that people are very trusting of each other here and never bother to lock their cars except in August when there is the danger of people trying to get rid of their excess zucchini crop. I looked forward to deeper experiences of these places of great beauty and being involved in life in a small town in Maine.

Chapter 3
Living Simply and Living So Well

In the schoolhouse, I knew I wanted to live in a very simple way—free from things I did not really need, junk, and clutter. I was also living in a smaller space. I had one large room compared to the five rooms I had in my house in Massachusetts. I only wanted what I could use. I wanted to have less and enjoy more. Worrying about excessive possessions could take up too much energy and time. I wanted to use all my time to experience nature and appreciate its endless beauty as much as possible.

I had no illusions about dressing stylishly in the forest where a casual dress style prevailed. I would have no need for silver eye shadow, but I did keep some handy just in case there was a chance to go out dancing someplace or to sparkle up my face on real gloomy days. I would have no need for fancy clothes. I could even wear different-colored socks with perverse delight. I did not scratch my brain figuring out what to wear. Practical clothes like jeans, layers of jerseys and turtle necks, insulated ski pants, thick sweaters and thick socks were comfortable and took the wear and tear from the physical work I was doing. I wore sturdy hiking boots year round as they were good in mud, snow, cold and rain and kept the bugs off my feet in the summer.

I had to become an official resident of the state of Maine, known as the Pine Tree State. I exchanged my Massachusetts license plate for the more elaborate Maine plate which featured a red lobster. This referred, of course, to the tasty and costly crustaceans that are hauled up out of the ocean along Maine's abundant coastline. I was living nowhere near the sea and my main notion of Maine was one of endless forests and zillions of trees. I did more than just get Maine license plates. I got vanity plates that proclaimed to everyone else on the road what I considered to be my favorite noun and verb: "wonder." Anywhere my car went, its "wonder" plates reflected my personal passion to appreciate all the beauty here in the forest. Soon a lot of people knew it was my car.

There were lots more bugs here than I was used to. Some were so tiny that they were called "no-see-ums." Hungry mosquitos were very prominent in the summer and part of the Maine experience. In the summer in the forest, I had to be careful not to breathe with my mouth open because the bugs were so thick it was easy to inhale them. Mosquitos could get very big in some of the swampy areas and there were some people who believed the mosquito should be pointed out as the state bird.

I was busy from the beginning making the schoolhouse livable after so many years of neglect. I lavished lots of care and attention on it as little by little I cleaned, scrubbed, repaired all the windows, put up shelves, made a closet and many other home improvements. As an artist I was in an underfunded profession and had never earned a lot of money, I was, therefore, very used to living well with limited financial resources and relying on my creative ingenuity. With my experience and skill, the abandoned schoolhouse was soon transformed into a comfortable and attractive living space. I certainly had a lot of confidence in the power and skill of my own hands. I found that I quickly overcame the challenges of physically surviving in the schoolhouse. I got good at heating with wood and soon prided myself on being able to start the stove fire with one match. I used oil lamps safely and delighted in their soft glow. I learned how to keep the lamps lit without getting even a speck of soot on their glass chimneys by keeping the wicks carefully adjusted.

From the beginning, things fell in place and I enjoyed living here and daily delighted in the rich gift of solitude that let me contemplate all around me. I heard only the sounds of nature: birds, a coyote's howl, the tiny feet of mice and the wind. I had room inside the schoolhouse to freely dance and spin on the solid maple floor. I never had this much open space in my previous house since the rooms were very tiny. I had brought my tap shoes and could make quite a racket that really must have confused the woodpeckers. As a natural soprano, I could sing as loud as I wanted here with no chance of disturbing anyone. There was no one else here and the nearest neighbor was a mile away. For the first time in my life I was really living alone—no roommates, lovers, or children. I could leave things where they were and they would be undisturbed. Books could just be left open to the page I was reading. I never had to nag anyone about leaving their dirty dishes in the sink. There was just me here and I could be a slob if I felt like it.

I knew there would be challenges in living without electricity, phones and running water. I had lived this way before when I traveled and lived in a VW bus for a year on the road in Central America. I had confidence that I could overcome the lack of modern conveniences. I did OK without an iron, toaster oven, hair dryer, but I did miss not being able to use my electric power tools like my circular saw and electric drill. The beauty of my eighteen acre forest was so immense and seductive. I knew that I needed to be here---with no distractions like a television to really enjoy it all. I could so easily hear the sounds of the birds echoing in this vast undisturbed space. There were no sounds of traffic to drown them out. When I first moved in, the silence was intense. I still, for a while, expected to hear the sound of a ringing phone. As I lived in the schoolhouse more and more, the silence was wrapped around me like a soft comfortable blanket.

Within a short time of residing in the schoolhouse, I was able to find ways to satisfy my basic survival needs of food, water and heat.

Water was always abundant and I had lots of ways to get it. There was a little brook that ran close to the side of the schoolhouse - less than twenty feet and this provided me with plenty of natural running water. Miraculously it never froze even in the coldest parts of the winter when its edges would be ringed with delicate lacy patterns of ice. I usually carried a bucket of water a day inside the schoolhouse to a cast iron sink that had no faucets. One bucket a day was all I usually needed for cooking and basic washing up.

In the warm weather, I would wash and bathe in the brook. It was hidden enough from the road so I felt safe about being naked. I made a small wooden platform that kept my feet from getting muddy. I hung my towel and toothbrush on a small sapling. I had a most ornate mirror as my face was reflected on the surface of the brook along with the tall branches of the surrounding trees. I also caught rain water in buckets placed under the roof. I kept extra buckets of water handy inside the schoolhouse in case there was a fire. In the winter when it was hard to go even the short distance to the brook or the spring because the snow was so high, I would simply scoop up kettles of snow and place them on the hot top of the wood stove where they would melt very quickly. I always had all the water I needed without turning on a faucet or paying a water bill.

Of course, having no indoor plumbing meant that I would have to use the outhouse. It was attached to the main structure of the schoolhouse by a narrow hallway. For this I was so grateful. I shuddered to imagine what going to the outhouse would have been like if I had to trudge through a howling snowstorm or a windy night when it would be twenty below zero. Still, it was pretty cold in the outhouse in winter. This did not matter when nature called. I got used to the outhouse soon enough. At first I kept instinctively wanting to flush it. My hand would reach for a lever that was not there, like trying to shift in an automatic car after driving with a shift for a long time. I would throw a handful of stove ashes, lime and old leaves and pine needles down the hole now and then to keep the smell down in the warmer months. After a while I myself never noticed the smell—although my occasional visitors might have smelled something objectionable.

When I moved in, the outhouse had a lot of loose boards below the seat and was in danger of falling apart. This was not my favorite place to work but I eventually got my courage up and replaced them. I covered the new boards with wire mesh to keep out the woodchucks that liked to chew through wood. The outhouse functioned greatly with no moving parts, a marvel of simplicity. I was so glad that I did not have to worry about frozen pipes as I always did when I lived in the Boston area. There were no pipes to freeze in the schoolhouse. Also whatever went into the outhouse just simply and naturally biodegraded over time and in place. No human waste traveled over long distances as it might with a public sewer system. For this reason, I thought the outhouse made good ecological sense. It made good economic sense, and for the first time in my life I had no utility bills. It was an amazingly free feeling to know that I could live here with very little money.

Since I did not have electric lights nor have any intention of getting them, I was careful to use to my advantage as much light as possible from the sun. This was harder in winter when the days were much shorter than in summer. Consequently, I did most of my drawing and painting during the day when there was sunlight. I read mainly at night since that was something I could do well by the light of a single oil lamp. In the winter, having enough light was a problem. By the second winter, I had cut through the walls of the schoolhouse and added three more windows which helped brighten the space.

Cooking was fun because I had lots of time to enjoy it and great views of the forest all around me. The challenge of not having a refrigerator led me to be more inventive. I produced some amazing meals such as stir fries and pasta with almost anything. I used food from my garden, including an abundance of squashes and tomatoes. I grew herbs such as basil and dill and had lots of fresh seasonings and fresh corn from a nearby farm. My kitchen area was very simple. In front of a window looking out to the brook, there was a dry sink of cast iron that drained to the outside through a hole in the wall. I installed a few wood cabinets I had found in the trash some years before. Then I made a checkerboard tiled countertop that was a real handy work

A Window to the Forest

surface. I screwed in hooks everywhere to hang things within reach and out of the way and built a spice rack. I continued to use a small two burner camping stove with small canisters of gas that lasted quite a long time. When I had the wood stove burning in the cold weather, I kept a kettle on the hot stove top and always had boiling water for tea.

In the warmer weather, I ate and cooked outside my front door on a ring of stones that formed a permanent campfire. Here I made use of twigs and deadwood which were in abundance as fuel. I soon learned to cook efficiently on the outdoor fire. It became very easy to boil water on the hottest part of the flame. I loved sitting around my fire in the summer dusk and watching hordes of bats fly out of the schoolhouse loft and then, counting the stars as they came out one by one. High up in the dark heavens, jet planes would silently plow across the night sky going to Europe. It was a relaxing way to cook and dine. Even Spam cooked on a wood fire and drained on some granite boulders tasted delicious. The smoke from the fire also kept the bugs away which I really appreciated.

I strove valiantly to keep my food safe and uncontaminated without refrigeration. I had no desire to re-experience food poisoning with which I had suffered several times in Latin America. I protected my food well. In the warm weather I would only buy the fresh fish or meat from town that I could use right away. In the summer the inside of the schoolhouse remained pleasantly cool and things like cheese kept well under an inverted ceramic cup. I also found that I could keep things cool by putting them in a screened box in the brook. In the cold weather with sub zero temperatures and plenty of snow and ice, a real refrigerator would have been redundant. In winter the shed area which was not heated was like a walk-in freezer.

Heat was my biggest necessity. I knew that I could freeze to death without it. But I also knew that I could make it through a cold night, if necessary, with no heat if I was well wrapped up in sleeping bags. As soon as the snow melted and the road was passable by truck, I was able to get a very necessary, new wood stove delivered. I chose a front loading stove with a glass door that would let me enjoy a view of the fire and flames. There were some pine trees that were too close to the roof for safety and they might have caught on fire from sparks flying out of the chimney. I knew that these trees were in the wrong place and I had to hire a logger to cut them down. The logger worked for a mere two hours and cut through the massive tree trunks as if they were made of butter with his chainsaw. The area around the schoolhouse looked as if a tornado had passed through as it had a jumble of trunk sections and huge branches scattered everywhere. Later I was able to make good use of the trunk sections to support a large deck. As a further precaution against fires, I had a clay chimney liner installed which could safely contain any flames that might be ignited from creosote build up. I invited an inspector from the fire department to take a professional look and he said it was fine.

I had never burned wood before, but I learned all I could about it. I made sure that my stove was securely connected to the chimney with no spaces that would let deadly gasses escape to my living space. I also made sure that I was burning dry, seasoned wood so that there would be less chance of a fire from the creosote buildup that could be produced from green, or unseasoned, wood. I learned how to progressively build a fire in the stove starting with crumpled newspaper, then twigs, then kindling from small pieces of hardwood or dried twigs and, finally, the big logs. I could adjust a damper that controlled the air intake to get the fire to burn fast or slow. I also had plenty of warm clothes, blankets, rugs and sleeping bags to burrow into. I stayed as warm as I needed to be. I was healthy and never even had a cold. I always kept a kettle of water on the stove to add some humidity to the air which otherwise would have become very dry.

The seasons cycled in their particular qualities and pleasures. In summer I enjoyed the warmth of the air and planted a garden. It was an amazing experience because I had never really had enough land in the other places I had lived. The house I had in Brookline, Massachusetts, had just a tiny walkway around it which was not enough space to grow anything except some tomatoes in containers. To the accompaniment of bird songs, I planted five fruit trees as soon as the ground thawed in early June. It was hard work digging the holes and I had to work around a lot of roots, but it was a joyous occasion to gently soothe and pat the earth around the roots of these new trees. I mounded dirt around the trunks and topped it with a mulch of dried pine needles and then made little circles of rocks around each tree. It might be a long time before they ever produced fruit but I was glad to have started the process.

In summer, I was surrounded by wildflowers and perennials that bloomed lavishly. The summer rain danced on the tin roof and was warm and good. My garden grew rapidly in July, the peak of summer. The days were long and the cool softness of dusk persisted until almost midnight as a special delicate twilight. Fireflies danced around like fairy spirits. Paradise was not perfect and the biting bugs could be pretty intense as they kept snacking on my skin. I scratched a lot and just got resigned to them. They did stay out of the schoolhouse.

Fall brought lavish displays of red, orange, gold, and magenta on the leaves as they changed to flaming colors and fluttered from the trees. Coolness turned to outright cold, the ground froze and I began to spend more time indoors but delighting in great views from my windows.

When the snow was finally down deep and thick, my lifestyle changed. It was the time for hibernating in the schoolhouse which was like a warm sheltering cave. I had plenty of wood, food, books, seed catalogs, art supplies, guitar strings, etc. I did inspired art with zestful energy. I stayed close to the stove, my hearth and the heart of the schoolhouse, for all the warmth I needed in the bitter cold weather.

At last, at the start of spring, I would walk around joyously in the afternoon savoring the new movements of buds beginning to burst from branches and new green shoots poking up through the melting snow. The brook would become very active with the increase of water as the snow and ice melted. The not so high waterfalls would become very boisterous. Tiny sweet wild strawberries came into bloom as tasty surprises almost hidden in the quickly growing wildflowers.

Being alone here I felt all this beauty so deeply. I was aware that the price to pay for all this exquisite solitude was loneliness. At this point in my life the price did not seem to be too high. I truly wanted a person in my life with which to share this beauty. The reality was that there seemed to be no one as free as me who could also survive up here and live away from a regular job. I often felt that it was only I who had somehow figured out how to live well here and have all this time to simply BE in the woods with no fixed agenda or schedule. Despite the loneliness, I know that I would not have traded this experience for anything else.

Another downside of living in such a remote area was random vandalism. If I was away, it would seem obvious because my car would not be seen. To intruders this would seem like an open invitation to break and enter. One day in late mud season when the road had just become passable again, I returned from town and saw that two of my front windows were broken from tossed beer bottles. This happened even though I had wire mesh over them. Once I saw that the back door was pried open. Miraculously nothing was missing. Another time, a glass cold frame I used for growing seedlings was smashed. It was discouraging to know that there were some people who would do this. I became a little afraid that they might try and bother me when I was inside alone. I had secure bolts on the doors and knew that there would be no way for me to defend myself against any sizable attacker. I also did not wish to have any firearm around. I believed that this schoolhouse was a place of peace and did not greatly fear anything here. When my car was parked on the ledge across from the schoolhouse, it was obvious someone was there and the vandals would not do anything. In winter I was very safe from intruders and vandalism since only I could get in and out by walking. No one was going to the trouble of walking through a mile of snow with evil intent.

The rich harvest of beauty I reaped as I lived in the schoolhouse was worth the hard work and outweighed the fears of living here alone. I was always reminded of a line from Sara Tisdale's poem *Barter*, in which she says, "…Life has loveliness to sell, buy it and never count the cost." These words were a constant refrain in my mind and I had even set the words to music that I played on my guitar.

Life here abounded in the richness of simple pleasures: washing my face in the brook with the reflections of the stars, the glow of moonlight, seeing from my window a deer leaping across the road with amazing grace, hearing the clatter of moose hooves from down the road, encountering delicate spider webs on trails blocking my path, the sound of the silence of soft falling snow and so much more. I felt the chance to live here was like winning a great prize and I had to be present to win.

Chapter 4
Scary Things

In this place of great solitude and beauty, there were two big scary things: fire and loneliness. I experienced both of these as real as I ever wanted them to be. Since I had no electricity or gas, the only way to heat the schoolhouse was by burning wood in a wood stove that acted like a radiant furnace. Wood was a plentiful and renewable resource here in western Maine. The cost of wood was inexpensive compared to oil or gas. Most people in my area got their own wood from the trees on their land and worked hard cutting it to the right size to fit in their stoves and stacking it neatly to dry. Wet, or green wood, was wood that had recently been cut and considered unsafe to burn because it still contained flammable substances that once vaporized could build up on the inside of the stove pipe and ignite. I knew that wood stoves could be dangerous because of the ever-present possibility of a fire from the accumulation of creosote or flying sparks and cinders. Since I was burning wood big time to survive the cold, I was naturally scared about flames and fire. In the area, it was not uncommon to hear stories of houses burning down quickly to the ground from out of control stoves. I had two scary incidents with my stove.

Not only was I a complete novice at burning wood, but I also had no running water that could put out a fire nor phone to call for help which could not get through anyway when the road was blocked with snow. I was as careful and took all the precautions I had heard about and read about. I made sure there was nothing flammable within four feet of the stove which was placed on a slab of stone-like material that had asbestos in it. There was another big slab of this stuff behind the stove. I always kept the ashes in a metal bucket where there would be no danger of a cinder igniting anything. I checked the stove pipe connections frequently to make sure they were secure so no toxic fumes would leak into the schoolhouse. I always made sure the damper valve was open so the smoke would go up the pipe and out into the sky. I was not going to take chances with danger.

Generally, things worked well between me and my stove. I kept it fed with seasoned seventeen-inch chunks of maple and oak and it heated up and kept me as warm as I needed to be. One afternoon in January, I returned to the schoolhouse after being away overnight visiting friends in town. It had been raining heavily on top of a thick layer of snow. I was wet and cold when I entered the big room and I got busy right away lighting a fire in the stove. Strangely, the smoke did not go up the chimney and began to pour through the stove door towards me. I was sure the damper was open but the thick black smoke just kept coming at me. The only thing I could think of was that there must be a big block of ice formed in the pipe from all the rain water that had fallen into the chimney in my absence when the stove was not in use. I ignored the smoke, opened the doors to the outside and got the fire going as hot as possible so as to melt the ice.

This seemed to have done the trick and indeed water soon started dripping out of the joints of the stove pipe into the room as the ice clog melted. It was scary with all that smoke but soon it disappeared. Slowly my forest home began to heat up. At four in the afternoon it was thirty-five degrees and at seven it was at last a comfortable seventy degrees around the stove. I resolved that this particular situation would not happen again and that I would get a chimney cap installed to keep out rain water in late spring when the road cleared and I could get someone with a tall ladder to get up on the roof.

The scariest thing that happened was a month later when I had an actual fire in the long slanted pipe that went up to the chimney. Late one afternoon I began to hear strange noises above my stove. It sounded just like mice scurrying back and forth inside the pipe. After briefly wondering why mice would be inside the pipe, I realized it was actually the sound of crackling flames. I was confused and smoke was again pouring into the schoolhouse. I did not even know where the fire was exactly. I had no water on hand and my fire extinguisher was frozen useless. I had fleeting feelings of sinking helplessness. It was dangerously cold, well below zero. I went outside for fresh air but I could not just watch my beloved schoolhouse burn. I was thinking briefly of escaping and just getting out to the nearest warmth which was a mile away through the snow to where I parked my car. The cold would kill me if I was motionless and not well covered. I was in a daze for a few moments. Yelling for help was useless. There was no one to hear or respond. No fire engine could ever roar down my road in winter.

Then I snapped out of this paralysis. I needed to know more about the extent of this fire. Smoke was still pouring out of the big room, but I saw no flames. I climbed the ladder up to the loft with a flashlight. The chimney was hot but I did not see any evidence that the fire had spread to any of the wood of the joists or rafters. There was no smoke up here. When I got back down to the main room, there was now less smoke. Ecstatically, I realized that the fire seemed to have burned itself out and my home-sweet-home was saved. The stove pipe was now cool and it seemed very clear that the fire had been confined to one spot inside it. I was very lucky.

Knowledge is power and I was able to figure out how the fire happened. About a month earlier, I had stupidly used some loose fiberglass insulation to plug some small leaks in the stove pipe. I had used a screwdriver to force the fiberglass into the tiny cracks. I did not realize that on the inside of the pipe it acted like a sponge and soaked up that flammable creosote that formed from the burning wood. At the time, it had seemed logical to do this since I knew that the fiberglass itself would not burn, but the accumulated creosote itself *did* burn. The fact that the pipe was angled might also have helped the creosote accumulate. I realized the error of my ways and decided I could take no chance and light the stove tonight since I could not be sure all the creosote had burned off. The only thing to do in order to feel safe was to completely take the pipe apart, clean it of any encrusted creosote and reassemble it. Only then would it be safe enough to light the stove again.

It was getting very dark and I knew I would have to wait until tomorrow morning to have enough light to do this properly. It was a long and cold night and the thermometer read a minus ten. I felt sure that the fire was gone and despite having no heat, I did manage to get some sleep huddled under many sleeping bags and a rug.

With renewed energy and the bright light of the new day, I got busy taking apart the stove pipe. I had all the right tools. I took the pipe apart with a small wrench. I used a wire brush, sand paper and steel wool and scraped the inside of the eight-inch pipe sections as clean as I could trying to get it down to the bare metal. Then, taking no chances whatsoever, I also cleaned and scraped the outlet at the top part of the stove that connects to the pipe. I needed to be sure there was no creosote in the pipes there that could catch on fire. My portable radio functioned perfectly and I managed to enjoy the sweet strains of classical music as I did this grisly work in the time of winter's deep freeze. My fingers felt like icicles and were taking a painful beating and my hands were beginning to look like hamburger. Slowly I managed to reassemble the pipe with sheet metal screws and made real sure that it fitted together better than before. I finished this task before noon and became covered with soot in the process. At last, I loaded wood into the stove and soon had a much-needed fire going. The schoolhouse slowly heated up bit by bit. After around three hours, the room temperature was comfortable near the stove and things returned to normal. I heated hot water and washed and soon was warm, clean and very much wiser.

Loneliness was the other big scary thing here. I set myself up for a lonely life by consciously deciding to live in this forest and escape an increasingly unnatural environment in the city. I also knew that I was here because of the more positive reason of wanting to experience this wilderness close up. I can't deny that it was often lonely. Dealing with loneliness was not as simple as fixing something mechanical like the stove pipe. I felt the presence of the big monster of loneliness hiding inside the old walls ready to emerge and pounce on my spirit with a growl as it took over the whole space here. The times of great loneliness were like dull thuds of the monster's heartbeat. Loneliness was painful. There was nothing eloquent to say about feeling like I was the last person left on earth hidden away here in the deep of winter especially when no one else can get here.

Marching to the beat of a different drummer who was probably myself was a risk. I knew I was different from a lot of other people. Who else would be so crazy to live out here, especially in winter when the road was blocked? Or who else would live here without electricity and a phone? I was not sure I would have wanted a phone or if it would have helped. I knew it was also possible to experience great loneliness in a crowded city. I refused to let loneliness level me and prevent me from enjoying the wonder of this place. Mainly I accepted that I had to be alone to be able to experience all this solitude and fantastic beauty. I painted, read, dreamed, sang and wrote. In writing I found companionship because I could talk to friends via letters and also with the hope of writing a book about my experiences here. I was not a total hermit and I soon became involved in interesting activities in town where I had made some friends. I survived extreme loneliness because I had hope that in the future I would have more times of being intimately connected to other humans and because I had faith that where I needed to be right now was here in this schoolhouse in the forest.

Chapter 5
Art from Wonder

My schoolhouse, sitting deep in the forest, was the best studio I ever had for doing art. Not only did I have a big open space with windows on three sides, but I was surrounded by inspiring and endless subject matter and so blessed by wonder, that quality of delight and mystical awe that can not be described in words. With the schoolhouse, I had been given the gift of a perfect art studio, complete with a big bed and continual access to coffee. I had great light from windows on three sides when the sun was shining and no interruptions. I could spread out my materials anywhere, let papers pile up on the floor, tape works in progress all over the walls, play the radio good and loud, sing at the top of my lungs, and even talk to myself. I could indulge in the fragrance of oil paints, linseed oil and turpentine and no one would complain of the odor. For many years, I had no choice but to work in cramped, small rooms and with very active twins underfoot. Now I had space to sprawl out in the big classroom of the schoolhouse. I had three large tables positioned around the room near the windows to see the great outdoors and to take advantage of the light. In the winter, I located myself closer to the wood stove for as much warmth as possible. Here I could fit my drawing board over a comfortable rocking chair I had found at the Albany dump. I parked myself there for hours lost in the compelling process of drawing and painting in warm comfort regardless of the temperature outside.

In my schoolhouse studio, I continued my lifelong passion to do art. I always wanted to do art ever since I can remember and was especially drawn to the excitement of colors. As a young girl, I would spend hours touching and contemplating many books of fabric samples in my father's cabinet making and upholstery shop. There would be so many shades and tones of colors like wine, olive, chartreuse, moss and apricot. Even the names of the colors were poetry. I loved the feel of the fabrics—especially the velvets and corduroys. I would amuse myself for hours by arranging the small samples in many different color combinations. I got another dose of color rapture when I worked in a drugstore selling cosmetics in college. I was astounded to see lipsticks in over sixty shades of red, each one a distinguishable difference from the other and with poetic names like Persian Melon, Peppermint Pink and Pango Peach. Eye shadow was also in a fascinating array of shades. I was able to tell the sixty shades of red apart. In graduate school, these tangible experiences of color led me to create paintings that were drenched in bold, brilliant hues of cadmium orange, thalo green, cerulean blue, rose madder and whatever else I could invent.

I had been an artist in the Boston area for many years. I taught art and actively exhibited in many places. I had some large mural commissions in the city of Boston but had worked mainly as a printmaker, specifically in silkscreening. I was in love with this way of producing original, limited edition prints. My zeal for silkscreening led me to write the book *Silkscreening*. I created many editions of prints and learned ways to do this simply and with a very minimum of technology which would have been too expensive for me. There was always magic in the process of pulling a squeegee loaded with ink across a screen stretched with silk to produce multiple impressions of an image. For me smell of the ink was like nectar to a bee. I especially loved the thick inks used in the printing process and being able to mix, experiment and invent all kinds of colors—especially variations of purple, magenta and cerise. In my art, I invented imaginary landscapes, fantasy flowers, apples that morphed into valentines reflecting experiences of my environment and life. I reached a high level of technical proficiency when I did a print that had eleven colors requiring great accuracy in the printing process to align the colors precisely.

Working in the schoolhouse took my art to a new level since I was so close to the natural world. For me, the schoolhouse was still a place for learning the living lessons of the forest that moved me to create new art on a daily basis. Each time as I would slowly wander in the forest, new and beautiful wonders would be revealed to me. I was amazed at the beauty and perfection of all things around me from the graceful precision of unfurling fiddle heads to the ruffled edges of the fungus growths on trees. Rich details of newly discovered colors and textures were more gifts given to me by the great artist creator above and I accepted them with gratitude.

Here I was rich with priceless experiences of beauty that no money could buy. Patterns everywhere delighted and inspired me as I observed the veins of leaves, the crystals of snowflakes, the so pointed textures of various kinds of pine needles, flower petals, the tiny multiple flowers of Queen Anne's lace, the fluffy seeds of dandelions and a world of so much more. Patches of lichens bloomed in perfect concentric circles on the weathered rocks by some kind of planed geometry. The changing colors of the sunsets were infinite iridescent light shows and touched with clouds like wisps of gold leaf. Each sunset was a unique treasure. The flickering shadows of leaves in the sun, moon shadows on the snow and sweet smell of blooming lilacs filled my senses with pleasure.

Each season had its certain splendors. In October, the fiery foliage and falling leaves of red, gold, orange was sheer visual magnificence. In the winter I became obsessed with painting the falling snow. My brushes danced patterns of dots of all sizes of white on a dark background. Snow falling on snow always amazed me. I watched for hours the crystal purity of snow and the way it fell silently out of the endless sky at night. Walking on snowshoes in the winter whiteness, I could see intricate patterns of the surviving dried weeds against the pure untouched snow. I observed the tracks of moose, deer, rabbits distinctly pressed deep into the snow and the light skimming tracks birds made. The aftermath of a fight was clear when I found a bunch of beautifully patterned grouse feathers so neatly stuck into the snow as darts hurled on a board. They had fallen this way as the predator killed its prey.

One bright sunny January day, I encountered a huge white rabbit, a snowshoe hare that changes its color in the summer to brown to better blend into the environment. It was about two feet tall and the biggest rabbit I had ever seen. It ran off as soon as it saw me. It was like a flash of a vision and inspired many paintings. This monster rabbit had the perfect ability to blend perfectly into the snow with its white fur just like a ghost.

I watched from my tables with drawing materials in hand, as spring came so slowly in subtle ways at first with delicate greenness and then at last with the bursting exuberance of blossoming trees. Summer was filled with the excitement of rapidly blooming flowers. White daisies dotted fields of green touched with the yellow blur of bobbing buttercups. Seeking a contrast of calmness I would often wander down my road and stare at the surface of Crocker Pond. As the endless dark ripples rolled towards me, I was hypnotized into a state of wonderful stillness accompanied by the jingle bell sound of frogs at dusk. At the pond, only a few jumping frogs would disturb my trance. I always hoped this would be the time deer would come to the water's edge to drink, but the deer seemed to keep out of my sight. Paradoxically, the more I tried to see them, the more I never saw them. I only saw these beautiful creatures by chance. Every day was a revelation of more beauty. Even the cloudy gloomy days brought dancing mists and raindrops suspended from pine and spruce needles like crystal globes. I was always eager to do art with all this inspiration.

Soon, I became moved to work artistically in the form of mandalas. These circular images have no beginning nor end and thus they convey a feeling of endless completeness. Mandalas have been used for thousands of years in mainly eastern religions as images to facilitate prayer and meditation. I drew intuitively and did not have a complex way of thinking about them. The mandalas were very organic growing things and I never knew how they would wind up until I was sure they were finished. The process of creating them was a real adventure. The paper was completely blank and pregnant with potential and the images emerged slowly. Shapes I had never seen before grew outward from a central point or inward from the circle's edge. I was moved to use images from nature like flowers, leaves, snow and rainbows as starting points in layers of color to create a new microcosmic world on the paper.

I was moved by the deep experience of a particular painting I did of a circular rainbow. I felt like it was a very personal image and I internalized it and it stuck with me. I used all the colors and had slow transitions from color to color. I mixed the paint in small quantities so that there were many hues in a flowing sequence. It looked like a slice of tree trunk with its annual rings. I sometimes would think of all the years of my life as the diverse and brilliant colors of a rainbow in ever-widening, rippling rings.

Here, deep in the forest, without the chaos of life as I often felt it in the city, I could more clearly hear and respond to the voices of inspiration. I had very few visitors, and no need to be somewhere else or at an outside job. At last, I had the needed solitude and time to just go deep into the world of my artistic imagination. I needed to be alone to do this. It was hard to paint when there are people around. No matter how nice they may be, occasional guests would always disturb my concentration.

I experienced needed creative growth when I began to work in my schoolhouse studio. I was now immersed in the deep beauty of nature. My inspiration was everywhere and closer to me than ever before. I knew that I needed a new way to express this. So I started working with new things that were not too evident in my previous work. I used tones, shadows, light and dark, and went deeper into the well of my imagination and used more time consuming techniques, slowly shading shapes and using innumerable progressive tints of paint. For the first time in my life, I had much of a major ingredient in creating art—unlimited time in which to work. I could freely follow my instinct and intuition. I began to really enjoy experimenting and working with new materials such as chalk pastels and pencils. I loved making scales of many tones of light and dark. It was exciting to see how shapes on paper could appear rounded and take on the quality of celestial outer space landscapes with amazing depth according to the way I placed the smooth gradations of lead pencils. I worked intensely with richly pigmented pencils blending colors and creating delicate veils of transparent tints.

Working in the schoolhouse, I managed, at last, to find my own way of working with the wild, slippery medium of watercolor. The more I worked with it, I realized that I did not want to control it. I got out of its way. I did not want to paint in a precise rigid manner. I began to enjoy splashing around in this medium and reveling in its wetness and exuberance. Being in my schoolhouse studio led me to these exciting changes and artistic growth as I strove to express in new ways my wonder and reverence for creation through my art.

Living well in the schoolhouse was also my art work. Art was everything and not confined to what I did with paint and pencils. I always remembered what Picasso had said when someone asked him what art was. His simple answer was another question: "What isn't?" Indeed, I have always known that there is the supreme art of living with attention to balance, contrast, harmony and unity just as there is in the design of an artwork. I arranged the schoolhouse to create a peaceful and efficient environment that was a place of beauty for me. My artistic impulse also led me in how I defined paths and planted flowers and created a vegetable garden. I arranged rocks on the granite ledge in front of the schoolhouse to form humanoid sculptures. I would stack rocks of varying sizes upon each other like the rock cairns used to mark trails on summits where there were often no trees. It was like making snowmen except these figures would never melt.

The creative urge was always with me. As an artist, I was always thinking of translating my experience and inspiration into the concrete form of art which was what I have to do and what I am called to do. I believe it is what I do best. I was always aware of the need to share my work but the reality of selling my work and connecting it with others has been very difficult, frustrating and seemingly impossible at times. At the schoolhouse I was remote from any art scene and removed from all that questing to be famous so I could sell my work. There were no local galleries in the area and absolutely no way I could have sold my work. So I did not worry about that so much. I just sunk myself into enjoying the joyous process of doing art in an atmosphere of lavish inspiration and creative solitude.

Being an artist here was very solitary. I knew that I did not create art that people here would find familiar and comfortable nor did I want to. Making art for me was a leap of faith into the unknown. It had to be an unpredictable adventure. Anything else would have been a false way of working and extremely boring. I knew that most people away from the urban centers wanted art they were comfortable with and art that was mainly representational. Artists who painted sailing ships, pets, horses and lighthouses had a chance of selling their work as these were popular themes in Maine. My art had no chance of being popular here. My art came from deep inside me and my own impulses. I was not interested in showing the precise position of a shadow or doing exact portraiture (which I could do). Being an artist was lonely even though the process of doing it was a joyful and pleasurable adventure.

I continually drank in the wonder of this forest. So many images of its beauty crowded my mind as an ever-playing movie. One afternoon in early April, I walked in slushy snow to Crocker Pond. I was alone but with my camera as my constant companion. The road was still blocked with snow so no other human had been here in months. The pond surface glimmered with large areas of thawing ice shimmering in the sun. These patches of bubbling foam contrasted with smooth mirror-like surface of the water. Small bushes bordered the pond's edge ready to bloom with buds. I circled slowly around the pond delighting in the patches of bright green moss and clumps of

Crocker Pond Melting in Spring

rusty pine needles now revealed as the melting snow shrunk. At the water's edge I could see fat tadpoles already come to life even this early in spring as they chugged through the cold water like helicopters. Around the shore birch trees stood tall in their intense silvery whiteness. The surrounding mountains were doubled in their magnificence as they were perfectly reflected in the smooth parts of the pond along with the vertical splendor of the birch trees. This beauty has no price and I know that if it is destroyed by pollution, bad logging practices, or being paved with asphalt, it will be gone forever. From living here and creating my own art, I know more and more of the details of this work of art we live on, this planet earth which is so very fragile and so beautiful and which I want to cherish and protect.

Chapter 6
Furry Roommates: Bats and Mice

Before I arrived, mice and bats had settled into the schoolhouse. They were pesky furry roommates who were not paying rent and who would not leave. I don't blame them for occupying the schoolhouse since this was the only standing structure they could have found within a mile radius. So I had no choice but to learn to surpass my dislike of these creatures and accept them and not think of them as pests. This was not easy because the schoolhouse had been boarded up and unoccupied by humans for many years. By the time I moved in, the mice had built cities in the walls and bats literally hung out in the rafters in a kind of rodent eminent domain.

I had spent a lot of time cleaning up mouse droppings which had accumulated in great quantity, enough to fill buckets. Mice had survived here very well. I could not imagine what they had been eating unless it was dried seeds and it seemed like they had been on the edge of starvation or their appetite increased when they saw me move in. These tiny rodents must have prepared for a feast as they instantly began to gnaw holes in my supplies of chocolate, rice, pasta, and grated cheese as I was deep in slumber. In the morning I would pick up a box of grits and observe a trail of it fall from holes the mice had chewed in a corner of the package. Trails of dry food crisscrossed my kitchen counter. Little piles of granola and flour littered my shelves and cabinets. These mice were having a feast every night. Soon I realized that I could not safely store food in anything cardboard or even plastic and began to use only glass and metal tins. When the mice were desperate they would chew anything even my candles and Dove soap. They were very active in the winter when the schoolhouse became their version of Florida and many of them moved back indoors into warm shelter. I like to think that we had a kind of truce. They stayed out of my bed and I agreed not to try and use nasty traps to catch or kill them. The mice mainly stayed out of sight and hidden in the walls when I was awake and I could hear them scurrying about in the walls. I still checked my bed clothes often just to be sure no mice were going to nest in close proximity to me.

My mice had their own social life and were quite busy at night when they thought I was asleep. Sometimes my sensitive ears could pick up the scratchy rhythms of their claws as they would dance noisily all around the tiled countertop in my kitchen area and knock chopsticks onto the floor with quite a clatter. I would yell at them to cease and desist as I drifted in and out of sleep. Once a cute mouse got stuck in a window between the glass and the screen. In the morning I got a good close look at his big black eyes, rounded ears and curly hairless tail. I liked him and spoke to him softly as I managed to scoop him into a glass jar with a lid. Then I released him in the forest on the other side of the brook and trusted he would not return to my personal space. I never could tell as the mice tended to look alike.

There were just too many of these tiny furry roommates. So I told myself they were OK. At least they were not big, biting city rats that carried bubonic plague. They were tiny country mice and I really could not smell them. Sometimes near dawn when I was half asleep, I would feel tiny hands and feet scurrying across my face. Reality was blurred and I can't figure out if I was dreaming or really imagining it. Later I had similar feelings about the bats.

Squirrels also tried to move in. Once I surprised a squirrel at high noon as she was effortlessly chewing through a Tupperware container filled with peanuts. I yelled at her and she vanished. There were also bigger things, like coyotes, woodchucks and porcupines, who were the scary mysterious critters with real big teeth that prowled about under the floor. I knew that they could not get into the main room and bite me so I did not worry about them so much. Little by little I sealed up the holes in the foundation with small rocks and wire mesh and this crawl space became less noisy as these interlopers began to find other places to live and rumble about.

One summer morning I noticed a huge bird flying into the schoolhouse through an open door. I was startled to see it hook onto the wall next to a painting and neatly fold its wings around itself like an umbrella. Then I realized it was actually a bat, something I regarded as a mouse with wings. Bats are creatures of the night, but this one was flying in the mid morning and must have been lost. I grabbed a broom and shooed it outside and started to be afraid of bats. A few months earlier when I had insulated the loft area, I had found out that bats were living up there hanging from the rafters. I was squeezed into the low space on my hands and knees between the joists and stuffing them with pink fiberglass insulation when I heard a squealing noise. I sensed something crawling around in the dark space. I used my flashlight to figure out what it was and saw a bat less than a foot from my nose. I screamed and shot out of there in a big hurry and didn't care about getting the rest of the insulation in place. Bats were the creepiest things I could imagine. Since that traumatic experience, I was usually careful to keep the door to the main room shut since I thought this would keep them out of my living space.

My fear and loathing of bats grew. On a very hot summer morning, I woke up and went to open the side door so I could go to the brook and wash up. My eyes were still groggy with sleep as I put my hand on the door knob. When I touched something soft, slimy and breathing, I saw to my horror that it was a bat! I ran out of the house barefoot in great haste. I could see the bat flying around in circles inside the schoolhouse and my whole body was tingling with fright. I wanted to get it out of there. When I finally got my nerve up to go back into the schoolhouse, the bat had disappeared from sight. I knew it was still there since bats are experts on hiding and can make themselves fit into the tinniest of cracks. I gingerly removed every picture from my walls and still couldn't find that bat. So I just tried to convince myself that it was gone and it seemed to be.

I was trying to be peaceful and not become completely obsessed with fear of bats. I did not want to hate them. I knew that they were beneficial to the environment and did some nice things like controlling the insect population by eating a lot of mosquitos. There were so many mosquitoes here that meant less of them to bite me. Late in the summer after I had moved into the new sleeping alcove I made, I began to hallucinate or sense that a bat kept flying by my face as I was sleeping. I could not imagine how Mice had gotten into the room. I had carefully filled every possible crack around the screened windows. This kept happening around the same time—at five thirty in the morning.

Finally I knew that I had to figure out the mystery of the bats. One morning I decided to actually awake. As I looked out the window next to my bed, I saw a swarm of bats flying right towards me. To my astonishment I found out that they were roosting within inches of my face. I had recently added new windows around my bed and had covered the outside space around the frame with black tar paper. I installed the wood trim very loosely so that rain would drain out of it easily and there would be less chance for rot to form. In my innocence or excessive logic, I had inadvertently created a perfect bat environment. The bats loved the dark spaces between the tar paper and the wood. Since I slept next to the window and could hear the bats, it was very easy to imagine that they were right on my bed and crawling on my face. Now I was able to clearly realize that all the bats were on the outside. They were crawling on the screen but the screen separated me from them and I was safe. Better than that I gained a perfect view of their return from a night of eating bugs or whatever else it is they do. For about ten minutes in the very early light of dawn, I could closely observe large numbers of bats of all sizes from my bed as they flew into their home next to the tar paper where they would fold their wings and sleep all day.

Amazingly I began to love my bats and bond with them. After all, we were fellow mammals. Now I knew their routines and could see them fly out at dusk as I sat around my campfire on the granite ledge. I began to look forward to their return around dawn. I started to think of them as friends. I learned a lesson in the schoolhouse that summer about how knowledge can eliminate fear.

Chapter 7
Winter: Moon Shadows on the Snow

Winter was my favorite season because the forest would be transformed with layers of snow and stillness. At last, the hunting season was over and there were no more rifle shots shattering the quiet of the forest that surrounded me. The hunters had roared away in their noisy pickup trucks with fresh-killed deer. My road became deserted and it was safe for me to go out walking in the forest without fear of being mistaken for a deer. Winter days grew shorter and the nights longer in the slow and sure momentum of the season. The forest was going to sleep as I felt and breathed the growing frigid presence of winter with its increasing cold. Soon thick snow would shelter the frozen earth with white softness. Ice would arrest all that did not move. Now I woke up to enjoy glistening fern-like patterns of frost that grew on the inside of my windows during the night. The cold air and moisture were the materials for these ephemeral works of art that nature created for me.

Shadows on the Snow

I had prepared well for the freezing weather and the long months of being snowed in. The Boy Scout motto which said "always prepared" in Latin was engraved on my mind even though I was the wrong gender for that group. My firewood was neatly stacked inside the schoolhouse in very accessible places—in the shed, in the main room and in the hallway to the outhouse. I had another big wood pile outside under a blue tarp, but I wanted to avoid having to go outside to get wood when the weather was severe. Around the schoolhouse, the smell of wood smoke from my stove perfumed the air with aromatic undertones that reminded me of the scent of sandalwood. All the leafy trees were completely bare except the low beeches. The fallen leaves were strewn about in heavy and stiff frozen clumps covered in a thin crystalline layer of frost and the earth froze hard for the big chill of winter and waited for its thick cover of snow.

Snow was the main attraction here. My warm rocking chair next to the wood stove was a ringside seat for the visual delight of the snow show. Snow had always fascinated me. I have been mesmerized by its pure, shiny crystal whiteness. As a child I often prayed for "snow days" when school would be closed because the amount of snow was considered sufficient to make it too difficult for students to get to the schools. I would eagerly listen to the radio to hear the list of school closings. When they announced Our Lady of Lourdes School in Bethesda, Maryland, I would shriek with delight and head outside to see the way my neighborhood was hidden by the snow as it changed into white rounded shapes. I would love to roll my snowsuit-bundled body down snow-covered hills as if I were a giant snowball.

I liked to believe I had grown up but I never stopped enjoying snow days. Through the long winter, I stared in peaceful amazement out the windows at the immense snow, softly, silently spinning down and so whiter than white. The snow kept falling and swirling as if from a great flour sifter in the sky. The entire forest would be transformed by the shimmering translucent veils of snow. It was as if heaven and earth became one since there was no way to tell what was earth and what was sky. The world was just endless, pure whiteness. The snow piled onto everything so gently. The rocky ledge outside the front door disappeared as if erased into total whiteness. When I walked as it was snowing, I enjoyed the feeling of the flakes gently landing on my face and melting. I even took out my reading glasses so I could see the unique crystal patterns of each flake, nothing less than a miracle of design beyond my comprehension.

Often the snow fell so gracefully that every single pine needle would be heaped high with inches of powdery light snow poised in a delicate balancing act. Snow snuggled into the thin close branches of shrubs like cotton balls. I was snowbound often and enjoyed the luxury of time to enjoy all this winter spectacle of exterior decoration in tones of white on white. As winter moved into February, the snow, layer by layer, rose over my knees. It was hard to believe it would ever melt as time also seemed to be frozen. I wondered if there would really be a summer.

The Brook That Never Freezes

If I listened closely, I could hear the lighthearted chatter of the brook alongside my schoolhouse. It was fed by an underground spring and because it was in perpetual motion, it never froze. I usually continued to haul my drinking and washing water from it. Despite the fierce cold, I enjoyed the quick trip to this beauty spot to get water because I could see how the edges of the brook had frozen into lacy scalloped patterns of ice and other formations that looked like clusters of grapes and stalactites. Nature had gone wild with its talent for ice sculpturing. I tried to maintain a path of packed snow so I could easily get to the brook which was only about twenty feet from the schoolhouse. However when the snow got really high, the path disappeared and walking to the brook became too much work. Then I resorted to drinking snow by simply scooping up kettles of it from outside my door and placing them on the wood stove to melt for all the water I needed.

In the deep chill of winter, I burrowed into my own comfortable, safe, private world inside my schoolhouse. It could have been well below zero degrees outside, but I felt snug inside the schoolhouse as long as I stayed within a four foot radius of the wood stove. On very sunny days, I felt like I was in the middle of a giant ice crystal that shot out rainbow rays. As the morning went on, the bright light bounced in and out through the windows and small rainbow patterns formed from the chandelier prisms that I had hung in my windows.

This crystal-like atmosphere was reinforced by the presence of a fringe of huge icicles, up to three feet long, hanging from the roof on both sides of the schoolhouse. The icicles had an ordered perfection because they were so evenly spaced and corresponded to the dips in the corrugated metal roofing material. Their radiance was blinding. I could see them easily from the inside as they glowed in the sunlight like a showcase of flashing diamonds at Tiffany's.

I also felt like I was in a cocoon of warm insulating snow as I was covered in blankets and sleeping bags, hibernating not outside like the bears around me, but inside near the comforting heat of the wood stove and holed up with plenty of books, blackberry wine, and munchies. I was resting, growing and ready to emerge as something else, maybe a butterfly or an improved version of myself with long flowing hair, when the earth became warm again. I would listen to the loud voices of the howling wind that swirled the snow outside into thick white clouds and read into oblivion, sheltered and warm. Even though the schoolhouse had been built over a hundred years ago, the original cedar posts and beams were strong and never even creaked.

I felt very safe inside but it was scary when I heard the avalanche for the first time. After a very heavy storm, snow had piled up high on the metal roof. One morning, the sun's warmth and the rising heat from my stove heated the roof and melted a bit of the snow and made everything slippery. This nudged the snow enough to send it all crashing down with a thunderous roar. It sounded like a train roaring right overhead. A mountain of snow shot past my window. I was stunned and scared that the ceiling was going to fall on top of me until I realized what was really happening and saw that there was no damage. There were encores of this raucous performance that became so familiar that I enjoyed it.

Keeping warm was always my main concern. My stash of dry wood was more than adequate and gave me the confidence that there was no way I would run out of heat as long as I had the energy to put wood in the stove and make sure the fire did not go out. In the dead of winter when the temperature could often plummet to a minus twenty, I dressed thickly like a snowman wearing a lot of clothing, including thermal underwear, purple leg warmers, wool sweaters, thick socks, and always a wool hat. I was always warm enough—especially if I kept moving or stayed close to the wood stove.

In the real freezing weather, I had to keep the stove fed continuously. The wood stove evolved into a portly beneficent idol to be appeased by feeding it offerings of dry hard wood logs when it got hungry. Therefore, it glowed and smiled upon me and kept me warm and I survived the cold very well. The wood stove had a glass door like a television screen. It was very entertaining to stare inside my stove at the innards of this idol which revealed dancing orange, yellow, and sometimes blue flames above the crumbling glowing coals, with structures that could seem like the lost city of Atlantis deep in the sea, with no commercial interruptions.

To keep real warm at night, I discovered the trick of heating up rocks by placing them on the top of the stove. Then I would wrap them in towels and put them in my bedding where they would radiate some much-needed heat. But in the extreme cold, and like a minus zero Fahrenheit, at two or three in the morning, I would wake up when the fire died. The cold would bite through my three sleeping bags and heavy socks like an iguana with sharp teeth, and relentlessly nip at my toes and wake me up. Going back to sleep was impossible until I could get the fire going again or my toes would become ice. It was something I really had to do, like answering the call of nature. Since I did not want to freeze, I would jump up in the very cold air, kneel in front of the wood stove idol, throw in some kindling and blow the cooling embers back to flaming existence with a long copper tube. I would load the hungry stove with as many logs as would fit. As soon as I had a roaring blaze, I burrowed back into my sleeping bags and was soon back to dreamful sleep.

The neat thing was that I did not need to heat the schoolhouse if I was not there. There was no need to worry about pipes freezing because there were none. Coming back into the unheated schoolhouse after a trip away or housesitting for friends in town was like entering a deep freeze. It was so cold that metal would shatter like glass. Once my cold hands dropped a metal knife on the hard maple floor. In amazement, I saw tiny splinters of the knife bounce off the floor. I noticed that my olive oil would congeal into a solid white mass. Wine fortunately never froze, but any water would be frozen solid. I learned never to leave any water around in buckets or pots when it was below freezing and the stove was off. I had to be very careful not to have any food in the schoolhouse during the winter that was in jars and cans. This was dangerous since they could freeze in the extreme cold and later as they thawed, the expanding water would cause the containers to burst and ruin the contents.

Having the food I needed was not a problem. I had made sure to bring in a sufficient supply of non-perishables while the road was still passable. When the road was blocked with snow, I simply backpacked in fresh meat, fish, fruit and vegetables. In the winter cooking was easy and I did not need to use my gas camping stove because I was able to do all of my cooking right on top of the wood stove. It could serve for both heating and cooking. I wrapped a chicken in aluminum foil and placed it on the logs inside the stove for a few hours as I was burning wood. It cooked perfectly and was delicious. A big kettle of water sat on top of the hot stove and the steam kept the air and my throat moist. In this way, I always had hot water ready for tea or coffee. There was a simple economy about being able to cook and heat the schoolhouse with just the wood stove even though it was not as simple as turning up the dial on a thermostat.

The birds also ate very well here. Their company was very much appreciated by me and I ensured this by feeding them lots of birdseed. I could almost tell time by the precisely scheduled way they would flock to my well-supplied feeders. The blue jays were the early birds and very aggressive. They were like my alarm clock. They used their size to bully the smaller birds. If there was not enough birdseed, the jays would pretend to be woodpeckers and start pecking on the bird feeder to get my attention. Doves visited, always in pairs, in late afternoon and they were so quiet I had to look hard to notice them.

The long months of winter were mainly spent reading, painting, drawing and walking around the forest. I was able to do art to my heart's content always with my inspiration right outside the door. I enjoyed reading tremendously, often by oil lamp and the schoolhouse was the perfect burrow for a bookworm like me. The Bethel Library in town supplied me with all the books I needed. Occasionally I would dig into the Sunday *New York Times* after packing it in. Reading it here deep in the forest was like reading news from another planet, enjoyable but unreal. The world of politics, fashion, business and modern life was light years away because I felt I was living a hundred years ago. For real frustration I would try and do the *Times'* crossword puzzle. It always stumped me since I tried hard but could never finish one. The newspaper itself was also excellent for starting a fire in the stove.

I could always listen to my radio which seemed to run forever on its batteries with amazingly good reception. Maine Public Radio was enjoyable company. Garrison Keeler's American Radio Theater could really make me laugh and sometimes cry. I could sometimes get my guitar in tune and play along with country western music performers. On Saturday afternoons, I would sing along with the Metropolitan Opera broadcasts that were exciting live performances from New York City. On weekdays, in the early afternoon, intellectually stimulating lectures on current issues and events from the National Press Club in Washington, D.C., fulfilled a need to hear human voices and keep in touch with the rest of the world as much as I wanted to be. International events went on without me, but I sure wished I could have been present as the Berlin Wall was, at last, physically dismantled. I was very glad to hear that news. I remembered how I had visited that massive wall when I was backpacking through Europe with my twins. I had been saddened to see such an abrupt division of the city and learn of the difficulties the wall caused.

Winter Reflections

Winter wonder reigned all around me. Solitude magnified the beauty of the forest that was so completely free of urban distractions. Though I was surrounded by snow on snow, it became obvious that there was nothing plain about the forest. The more I looked, the more I saw. I had the time to appreciate subtle distinctions and could now clearly see the rolling forms of the land that were no longer hidden by the dense foliage of the undergrowth. The white paper-like bark of the birch trees glowed against the snow. On its thin finger-like branches stretched to the sun, I could see the new buds ready to swell in spring. Tracks, clumps of feathers and sometimes blood in the snow told stories about who was chasing whom. Coyotes, birds, rabbits, foxes left their footprints etched in the snow like letters stitched in a sampler. I often saw deer tracks but could never see the deer who were yarded down in their secret thickets. Sometimes the fat grouse would be startled as I unwittingly chugged by their nests hidden in thick tangles of brush. They would threaten me with a thunderous clatter of wings that was more sound than fury since we both knew they were not high flyers that could escape my intrusion near their ground-level homes.

There was easy access to cross-country skiing here as long as I stuck to a road. I just had to step outside my door, click into my skis and glide away. If the snow wasn't real high, I could explore some of the many logging roads that ran off the main road. Often I skied to Crocker Pond which was totally frozen over into an expanse of pristine, snowy whiteness broken only by tracks of birds. Sometimes my neighbor, Laurie, from a mile away would come by on skis and have tea. I really enjoyed her company even when she had her dogs who would chew my slippers as if they were their favorite bones.

The forest itself was too rough for skiing so I would walk or snowshoe. It could be very slow going after a fresh thick snow because I could not simply move my feet forward. It was like walking in cake mix. I would have to keep lifting my feet high to clear the depth of the snow with each step. Sometimes if the top layer of the snow had melted and then glazed over as thick ice, I got lucky and could easily walk and slide on top of the snow which supported my weight.

I never saw another human in the winter forest. It was like being the first person on the moon or the last person left on earth. I had no doubt that this beauty would exist if I were not there to experience it. The time of sunset was magical. As I walked deep in the forest in the late afternoon, the sun flirted in and out of silver gray clouds and gilded the tops of the tall pines and spruces only hitting the tops of the trees. It almost looked like a theatrical effect but I felt like I was in a sacred cathedral with stained glass because I was in such awe of something divine and bigger than me. A skilled lighting technician up above in the heavens was turning dimmer switches back and forth to create dazzling special effects. The bare branches of the maples and oaks twisted up to the heavens in a symphony of swaying lines. It seems that the tip of each tiny twig picked up the dying day's golden light from the west. The sky at the end of the day often glowed from yellow to orange to pink. On cloudy days, the sky was a subtle weaving of silvery grays that slowly merged into the darkness of the night.

The price for following my dream to this terrestrial ecstasy could seem like loneliness. I was able to be in the forest enjoying its beauty but I still wished for someone to share it. Inside the schoolhouse, I was alone here with only the mice and the ticking of my clock and the logs crumbling into embers. I would fantasize about having any kind of warm mammal to be with or closer friends who were not so far away. I knew I was well off the beaten path living alone here but the lure of the forest had been irresistible. For close to five months, the high river of snow blocked the road and only skiers and walkers like me could get in and out. At times, I imagined the snow on the road to be as high as the Hoover Dam and just as insurmountable. I really had wanted a slower social pace than I had in the city where I was always going to openings, plays and concerts, but I wondered if I had gone overboard on the quest for solitude. I wondered how long I would stay here under the spell of all this natural beauty which I loved so much.

As I accepted the loneliness and winter darkness, I came to really appreciate people and light. Other roads besides mine were covered with snow and I really had to think seriously about going anywhere frivolous or just driving around the area. I was in town at least twice a week and I looked forward to going to the library and then to choir practice on Thursday nights and church on Sundays no matter how high the snow was.

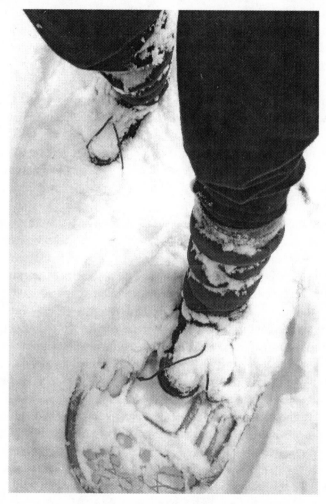

Slow Snowshoeing in the Thick Snow
As winter ground on, the snow accumulated into higher levels.

Usually I could walk to my car on the plowed part of the road in about a half an hour. My car would start right up and I would be on my way to town. I set out one morning after a heavy all-night snowfall to get to a meeting in Bethel. The snow was over my knees and I wore sunglasses to avoid being blinded by the brilliance of snow and sun. I left my schoolhouse around nine and, even with my snowshoes, it took me two and a half hours to reach my car. It was the longest road walk yet and I had to stop and keep adjusting the bindings on my snowshoes because my boots kept slipping. When I finally did reach my car, it was completely buried in snow from the plows. I spent another hour shoveling it out and then I stalled the car trying to pull it out onto the road over too much snow. I walked to a neighbor and called a tow truck which eventually pulled me out and set me back forty dollars. I learned from this not be in a hurry and rev up the engine to get over thick snow and to just keep shoveling until there was sufficient clear space for the car.

Walking on the snow-covered road came to be my most powerful pleasure as I grew to enjoy what I originally thought would be a hardship. I had thought I would hate doing this and that it would be something I was doing simply because of the necessity of getting back and forth. The more I walked alone on that one-mile stretch of thick snow, the more I passed from resignation to sinking into the experience. I came to appreciate more and more the splendor and silence of winter and the glowing sheer whiteness of the snow. It was so exhilarating to walk during the day under a pure blue sky that I was inspired to sing opera at the top of my lungs. Walking at night was different. I needed to be quiet to feel safe. With the moon and stars so clearly above me I enjoyed a mystical experience and a repetitive meditation on winter. So many times as I walked in the cold night, my spirit drank in the brilliance of the moon and all the dark shadows it cast on the snow. If I walked backwards, I could see my own shadow and as I looked up I saw the tops of the trees in lacy patterns.

I would walk the road on Thursday nights as I came back from choir practice with a backpack full of groceries and fresh library books. The stars glistened like diamonds with no competition from any electric light. They seemed to be so close that they were fruit on the bare tree branches that I could reach up and pick. The deep indigo infinity of the universe was a priceless marvel as I could see the Milky Way so clearly with my bare eyes.

The looming, dark silhouettes of the evergreens that made part of the road seem like a tunnel became familiar landmarks. There was one certain spot where a stand of white birch glowed luminescently in the blueish moonlight. I also knew just where I would hear the slight rustle of dried leaves still hanging on the low, beech trees. I could distinguish shades of gray at night which were enough to guide me. I never felt the need to use a flashlight even though I carried one. Moonlight and reflections from the snow were all the light I needed to walk in this special peaceful quiet beauty of the winter night.

The sound of my boots told me what kind of surface I was walking on. It could be loose snow, packed snow from a skier's tracks or ice. My body made the necessary minor adjustments when my feet would feel the slipperiness and signal caution. My power of balance had been very well developed from lots of figure skating. Only once did I have a problem. It was as I was coming back, well after midnight, from a New Year's Eve party in town. It had been raining all afternoon and a thick layer of ice froze over the snow. Walking tonight seemed impossible and scary. The road was more slippery than an ice rink. I had to navigate a lot of the uphill parts of the road on my hands and knees. I pretended my body was a sled and just slid down the hilly sections and crawled a lot. I suffered no bad effects because I was well padded with clothing.

As often as I walked the road, I never encountered any other person or animal. Anticipating the comfort of my schoolhouse, I would walk on and on at night in amazement, peace and gratitude that I could experience the beauty of the winter night. When I would hear the welcoming familiar gurgle of the brook that never freezes, I knew that I was near my schoolhouse home. So soon, I would light the wood stove, carefully slip into my sleeping bags and soon be deep in slumber and many dreams.

Winter slowly wore itself out and the days grew a little longer. I began to have more daylight and noticed that I could light the oil lamps later in the afternoon. Different bird songs began to fill the air as the birds returned from the south. Colorful seed catalogs mysteriously showed up in my mail which I poured over with great zeal. I planned the garden I was eager to start even though I could hardly believe all this snow would melt and the ground would thaw. Winter wound down exhausted from its bravura performance as spring waited in the wings to wake up the earth with new energy.

Chapter 8
Spring: Thawing Snow
and New Greenness

Here at the schoolhouse in Mud City, the drama of spring began with snow still covering the land. Each day another pinch of darkness diminished as the days got longer. The doves started their gentle cooing that stood out as soothing music for my spirits that had long been cooped up from winter.

I could feel how the earth began to warm up slowly. One morning, I was delighted to realize that I could sleep the whole night through without having to reload the stove with wood when the fire went out. It was getting warmer, degree by degree, and I did not need to keep lighting the fire in the middle of the night. Soon, I did not even have to use the wood stove at all at night. The snow that was piled up over my window sills slowly melted and receded inch by inch. Snow-buried lawn furniture emerged back into existence. I began to see again how plushly the forest floor was carpeted with scraps of a rich tapestry of pine needles, twigs and last year's dried leaves. There was an energy in the air with the new smell of damp dirt, springy bright green moss, and balsam fir. The stone walls seemed to wear wigs of red pine needles once the snow melted off them.

Soon there was the sound of dripping running water everywhere like a gentle syncopated drumbeat. Crocker Pond began to melt into bubbling foam as it was then transformed into smooth clear water like a mirror. The road in front of the schoolhouse remained snow and mud blocked into May and I still walked back and forth between my schoolhouse and my car. Spring included "mud season" with mud everywhere. The back roads around Bethel were slippery and thick with mud from all the melting snow. When I drove, I tried to stick to the higher dry spots so I would not get stuck in the mud and have to get towed out.

Early spring was maple sugaring time, an endeavor I had never before experienced when I was in the city. Small metal tubes were attached to the trunks of sugar maple trees to tap the sweet sap that flowed into five-gallon buckets. When enough raw sap was collected, people would collect themselves into the sugaring shacks where the sap was slowly and carefully boiled down to produce sweet maple syrup. Sometimes people spent a lot of time in the sugaring shacks and socialized while waiting for the sap to boil down to the desired color and consistency. The boiling sap had to be carefully watched. This could sometimes take two weeks or more. My neighbors up the road had a farm and had always made syrup and I enjoyed a warm afternoon there listening as they talked about the old days in an atmosphere steamy with the sweet smell of boiling sap.

With spring, I slowly emerged from the hibernation of my winter cocoon in the schoolhouse into more time spent outdoors in the fresh, exhilarating air. My body was moving more as I did more physical work which was a good balance to my sedentary life in winter of doing art and reading all the books I could. I used wood scraps and made paths so I could get around easily and not sink into the mud and get my feet wet. I wasn't really trying to make it all look neat and tidy. I was just trying to have a comfortable way of moving around outside. I especially wanted a dry path to the brook since I got my water out of it every day.

There were always plenty of things to fix in the schoolhouse. I did not go overboard on changes, but my head swarmed with ideas for home improvements as I was blessed with strong building and nesting instincts. Any carpentry here was very challenging since I did not have electricity and could not use my power tools. My first big project after getting all the windows functioning was to build a deck where I could just sit, read and nap. There was, however, a limit on my aspirations since I had no desire for plumbing or electricity nor could I afford them. The clapboard siding needed paint but I was content with that rough way it looked.

My deck went up very quickly. I had plenty of the big sections of tree trunks from tall pines that had to be cut down because they were too close to the chimney. They came in handy as supports for the floor joists. The rough trunks were massive but I was able to roll them alongside the back of the schoolhouse. Using my legs to push, I was able to lift the trunks upright and position them into the corners of a twelve-by-twelve-foot deck. I painted the tops of the trunks with wood preservative and covered them with tar paper so there would be less chance of the wood rotting. At the lumber yard in Bethel, I made sure to pick out the right lengths of wood so I did not have to do any sawing at all. I just nailed a platform of joists on top of the pine trunks and then nailed on the long planks of wood. The deck was very sturdy and it was a satisfying feeling to take a pile of loose boards and a few hours later hammer it into a real structure that I could jump around on. I just built it without a building permit. I was living in a remote area and no one could have been able to see it from the road. I positioned the deck about four feet from the side door of the schoolhouse. I was hoping that the distance would help prevent snow and rain from the roof from running onto it. I made an easily removable gangplank to connect it to the side door. I really enjoyed that deck and it was the perfect place to hang a clothesline, relax and stare out at the forest all around me.

I built a closet in the big room of the schoolhouse and the clutter of clothes disappeared. Then I really got ambitious and carved out an eight-by-eight foot bedroom in half of the shed area. I hired someone with a generator and a long-bladed electric saw to cut three openings for new windows and a big opening from the shed into the main room.

The rest of the wood I managed to cut by hand. It was very inexpensive to make this new space because I used wood, old windows and doors that I had found in the trash. I insulated the walls and the floor and this became a very cozy place to sleep, read by lamplight, watch the stars and await the returning of my bats at dawn.

I continued working and cleaning inside the schoolhouse. I thoroughly scrubbed the hard maple floor many times and it began to have a nice clean glow at last. I painted some of the interior bright green and outlined the windows with bright pink which made the inside seem brighter. Ignoring the roosting bats, I worked up my nerve to climb the shaky ladder into the loft and cleaned out a lot of stuff—including some shutters which I fixed, painted and hung on the windows.

It was not all work here and I always had time to wander around the forest which was now easier as the snow melted. Trying to follow the official boundaries of my land gave me a sense of just how big eighteen acres was. I would start by walking up the road to a marker tree painted with yellow slashes. Then I followed the trees that were tied with pink surveyors' tape in a straight line. I crossed my brook and went through wild forest, up and down small hills and across the right-of-way which was a logging road. Then I pushed through thick stands of maple and oak saplings and connected with the intersection of the old Mud City Road. This was the southwest corner of my land indicated by a pipe with a lot of slashes of red paint and a Forest Service marker which indicated an edge of the White Mountain National Forest. I would then head east on the Mud City Road and follow a long stretch of stone wall, past the cellar hole and soon the back of my schoolhouse would come into view. Since I was a real slowpoke, it often took me about two hours to walk around the land which seemed vast. It was easy to get lost but I loved being totally in the forest.

One spring afternoon before the snow completely melted, I decided to follow the old Mud City Road west as far as I could. I went way past my property line and then through an area that had recently been logged. The road was very overgrown and barely still visible as it led over a small river lined with smooth boulders. I made a note of the sandy spots on the river thinking it would be nice to come back there in the summer and swim in its cool waters. I crossed the river on a still sturdy old bridge and continued on the faint road along its bank. I passed a few startled grouse and eventually began to see lots of people tracks on the still-lingering patches of snow. For a while I could not imagine how people had been able to get here. I looked around and saw a big house that looked familiar and I realized I was almost at the school bus turnaround on Flat Road. Then my suspicion about this road connecting to the main road was confirmed and I was back on my road going towards my home. So the mystery of the Mud City Road was now solved. It was a loop and my schoolhouse was at one end and the main road was at the other end. It was obvious that no one had driven on the Mud City road in many years and it was about to disappear in the overgrowth. I was glad I was still able to follow it.

The days grew longer in the increasing sunshine and I no longer had to scramble so much to take advantage of the light to draw and paint. Hibernation was over and the weather began to be more pleasant as the forest creatures were out and about now. I often saw moose dancing in mud puddles. The deer were always shy and liked to be hidden away in deep thickets chewing all the tender leaves they could reach. Bright red-crested woodpeckers showed up frequently to dig in dead wood for insects. One day a woodpecker mistook my stovepipe for a tree and created a horrendous sound when he tried to peck into the metal. It sounded as if someone was banging with a metal pipe.

One day I had the company of a fellow sun worshipper as I sat in the new warm sunshine on the granite ledge outside my front door. A black snake had also been attracted to the warmth that felt so good on my face. The snake was about three feet long and from time to time until the fall, I would see it slither out from under the schoolhouse to the ledge where, like me, it loved to soak up the sun's rays.

As I slowly walked in all this beauty, I kept my eyes, ears and all my senses wide open. I heard the quiet as well as the music of birdsongs, the sound of green things growing and the whispers of the wind. There was much to touch also as I would tenderly run my fingertips over velvet moss, rough bark and stone and feel their aliveness. My feet bounced on the springiness of massed pine needles and the squishiness of mud. The abstract shapes of patches of snow that changed as they melted and faded away were fascinating modern art.

Fiddlehead Ferns Coiled to Burst into Leaf

I was poised to notice the tips of plants beginning to push through the now-soft earth as their stored golden greenness bubbled forth. In the nearby orchards, the sky would be suddenly filled with apple blossoms. The birth of masses of new leaves as they slowly unfurled from the buds in spirals to fill the sky was truly a marvel of nature's engineering. I would enjoy surprises of pure white Indian Pipes, a low plant unusual in that it has no chlorophyl, puffy pink Lady Slippers which are a species of orchid and so much more as I wandered in the forest in wordless amazement. After long stretches of slow and soft spring rain, I smelled the forest glowing in the sunshine reflecting off the new leaves. I was truly in an earthly paradise and blessed by wonder as the miracle of spring and new growth had renewed the barren once frozen earth.

Chapter 9
Summer: Long Warm Days of Beauty

At last, there came a day when it was actually hot and sweat dripped off my face and I realized that summer was finally here in all its splendor and languid warmth. Wildflowers bloomed with extravagant grace and were in such abundance that their lavish colors took my breath away in pure amazement. The sun danced all over the land as I reveled in old meadows that were filled with bright white yellow-eyed daisies, yellow black-eyed Susans, orange devil's paintbrush and my favorite member of the carrot family: the so-delicate Queen Anne's lace. Summer was the time to lie on my back in fields and on the granite ledges and watch the clouds dance by like popcorn bursting in the deep blue sky. I basked in the long-awaited sunshine through long lingering days to the accompaniment of bird songs and crickets, and the sweet pastel-colored dusk that merged with the short night. The living was relaxed and easy and some friends even came to visit.

By the end of June, the thick spring mud dried up and everything began growing wildly. I endlessly enjoyed rambling around my eighteen acres where I could still get delightfully lost. I often carried loppers to cut the brush and try to keep a path clear through the countless small seedlings and saplings that just kept sprouting up. The overgrowth was so thick that it was hard to believe the deer and moose could get through it. I had often seen them simply disappear into the forest after staring at me for a while.

My eighteen acre forest was filled with so much wonder and mystery to see, to hear, to feel and explore. Every day I encountered a new hill, rock formation, exotic butterfly, fresh blossoms of trillium, exuberant ferns or strange flowers I had never seen before. The trees were now in full leaf and the sunlight filtered into the forest in all shades of glimmering green especially after the rain. The small waterfalls from my brook created a delightful sound that reminded me of the sweet tones of marimba music I heard so often when I was in Guatemala. The smell of balsam fir, lilacs and roses wafted into the moist, hot air of summer.

I continued working inside and out. In the Albany dump, I had found a small chainsaw that would not require electricity. I took it to a repair shop to find out for sure that it worked. I was looking forward to using it to cut up a tree that was growing out of the foundation. I had seen other people using chainsaws and it seemed easy enough: just pull the cord hard and it was supposed to start right up. Other people, men, for instance, had no problem doing this. I did not have great upper body strength and I never could pull the cord strongly and fast.

I was struggling to start the chainsaw one hot July afternoon. I tried hard but it was just impossible for me to get that thing going. It's not that I am weak—but all my strength is in my legs and thighs. I tried tying the starter cord to my boot and kicking to start the chainsaw. I continued to have no luck. I was mad and swearing a lot, and after all, there was no other human to hear me. Then a car pulled up and these two older women introduced themselves as Ruth and Grace, my neighbors. They had been out joy riding and were curious about who was living in the schoolhouse. I invited them in for tea, and despite my frustration with the chainsaw, I enjoyed their company and conversation. I played them a song on my guitar and that also seemed to calm me down. These women were very friendly and I got to know them more as I lived here. After they drove off, I faced the reality of my weak arm muscles and resigned myself to the fate of not being able to use a chainsaw like the big guys. Later I took it back to the dump so someone else could have it and I gave up my dreams of cutting up wood quickly. I used a bow saw and cut a lot less than I thought I would. Of course, this was a lot more quiet than a chainsaw that made a fearful noise which I hated.

In the good weather of summer, I continued making improvements to the schoolhouse. I bought an elegant, old oak door with glass panes from a man named Bunny on Route Two who had a perpetual yard sale at his house. I installed it in the schoolhouse where it opened into the shed. I had more light inside now and since I could see out to the front door, I felt less claustrophobic inside. In the interest of better living, the attached outhouse was insulated with thick sheets of Styrofoam that I had salvaged in Boston. Then I made a screen for the window and hung a small battery-operated light. It was comfortable there and you could even read. I no longer missed modern plumbing and had developed a diminished awareness of the odor from the outhouse.

Because my schoolhouse was right on the road, I decided to put up a fence so I would have more privacy. Now that the road was very drivable, cars were more frequent especially as they drove to the campground at Crocker Pond. I always heard the vehicles slow down as they came near. I could sense that they were curious about who lived here.

I used the remaining large tree stumps and branches from the pines that I had to have cut down. I spaced the thick trunks about every five feet and nailed branches onto them horizontally. My rudimentary fence looked like it belonged there about a thousand years ago to protect livestock. I was able to use the materials I had on hand and the fence did not cost me anything except the price of nails. With the fence up, I felt less conspicuous.

Gardening was an essential summer delight. In early June, when the ground thawed at last, I cleared out a small area in a sunny spot and planted a garden with tomatoes, beans, squash and lots of herbs. Working in my garden felt natural, good and right. I sang in joy as I dug, planted seeds and gently patted soft earth around them. I had an innate need to garden which reinforced a natural connection to the land and mother earth.

Summer was a time of a wild profusion of flowers. There was always something in bloom and lots of purple flowers. The lupine grew by leaps and bounds. Friends taught me a lot about the ways of nature. My friend, Shirley, pointed out to me how a drop of water always gets trapped in the center of radiating leaves of lupine like a glistening diamond. My days in summer were filled with such beautiful surprises. Shirley lived up the road about three miles away. She was also an artist and for me a dear kindred spirit. She died very suddenly and was greatly mourned and missed by her family and many in the community. I still think of her often and her love for the beauty of nature and especially when I hear tree creaks, the sound made when heavy branches of different trees rub together.

My schoolhouse soon abounded with hardy perennials in addition to the lilacs, roses and lilies that were already there. My good friend, Peter Lenz, from nearby Norway, Maine, kept me well supplied with amazing perennials from his own extensive garden which we planted around the front door of the schoolhouse. Through him, I learned about flowers I could never imagine such as phlox, lung wart, columbine, bachelor's button, Job's tears and bee balm. The flowers were hardy and flourished. The neatest thing was that they survived the winter and would keep on coming up automatically, year after year.

Peter's visits were always pleasant surprises, more so since I had no phone. More than once, when I came back to the schoolhouse, I would notice a small cairn of rocks that had been built in my short absence. Without a doubt, I knew, as sure as if he had left a calling card, that Peter had been by. Peter is a historian and is always researching and writing books. He knows so much about the area and is a true well of information on local history and his enthusiasm for his subjects is contagious. Sometimes I did not see Peter for a few months and I knew that he was off in Portland trying to earn some money by doing house painting and carpentry. There was not much paying work here in Oxford County. Although Peter was a passionate historian and writer and totally immersed in his work, he had to do something that paid money from time to time. Being an artist, I understood this well. I often had to get paid work such as working as a substitute teacher because it was impossible to survive solely from the sale of my artwork.

A Stone Cairn, Peter's Calling Card

In the warm embrace of summer and right before my eyes, everything flourished in my garden of Eden. There was enough rain and I always had the nearby brook for extra water for the plants. The day lilies bloomed almost continuously in July. I could see the closed up flowers open up in the morning sun. Hummingbirds with breasts of green gold appeared out of nowhere to nestle their whole body into the cup formed by the petals of the lily. Their long beaks penetrated deep into the flower for its sweet nectar. Soon the red-magenta bee balm flowered attracting even more humming birds.

The intensity of growth of everything around me was as if the forest was cooking a soup of compost, mulch and mold. The leaves of the maple, oak and birch grew to maturity and filtered the sun to cooling shade. The new growth of the fir trees showed forth in bright light green needles sparkling in the sun. Newly formed branches reached outward and up. From a forester, I learned the differences between evergreens by their needle patterns. On a fir tree, the needles are lined up flatly along the spines of the branches. On a spruce, they grow in a rounded pattern. On a red pine, the long needles cluster in groups of two. On a white pine, they group into fives. I learned how the leaf of a sugar maple is smoother than that of a red maple. The more I learned about the complexity and uniqueness of trees, the more I loved them.

Although it was usually very quiet here, some sounds had to be explored. At first when I heard a loud crunching of twigs, I expected that I would soon see a big animal like a bear, moose or even an elephant. Then, to my relief, or maybe disappointment, all I saw were chipmunks chasing each other with a loud clatter and whirling chattering sounds. I could not believe how a cute, tiny, striped chipmunks could be so noisy.

The summer weather was generally pleasant although there were a few thick heat waves that slowed me down. Sitting in the brook was a great way to get cool. I would not work outside in the peak of the day's heat and stayed in the cool comfort of the schoolhouse. When there were long spells of gloomy rainy days, I would especially enjoy my big stashes of library books. I also made sure I stayed inside if there were thunderstorms.

In the early summer ticks were a problem. I wasn't too aware of them at first as I rambled through old meadows in thick grass where the deer ticks abounded. The tiny insects were sneaky and they would grab on to my skin and I would not feel a thing nor notice they were there. After discovering enough ticks by accident on my body and not wanting to again experience that creepy feeling, I became properly vigilant and would check everywhere on my body for them before going to bed. I was scared because I knew they could carry Lyme disease which causes fever, chills and worse things. I worried especially after I found a bad-looking red circle the size of a quarter around a spot where I had picked off a group of five ticks who had probably been hiding on my skin for some time.

The only thing bad about summer were the bugs which were a constant topic of complaining conversation. The black flies, often called no-see-ums, were a grand nuisance and very thick all summer. They would swarm all around me when I was outside. I tried many brands of repellent without much success. I rubbed in lots of Skin So Soft, a lotion made by Avon that many people found to have excellent qualities as an insect repellent, to no avail. Even wearing a mosquito net did not help much. I was, however, able to relax around my campfire where the smoke kept them away. Mosquitos were everywhere and always biting me. My body was a magnet for them. Around the end of August as it got slowly cooler, the bugs finally started to disappear and I could again breathe with my mouth open outside.

Despite the bugs, I still enjoyed wandering around my neighborhood of Mud City. In the delicate after-dawn coolness, I would meander along stone walls and weave around trees finding new hills and thickets. I was always curious to find out where the many old roads led. Some trails near the old logging town of Gilead led me to patches of sweet blackberries. I stuffed myself with them and then waded in a cool green river shaded by spruce trees with brook trout nipping at my ankles. This was the good life I had dreamed about.

The long stretched-out days of summer were especially suitable for hanging around ponds at dusk. The tranquility of the water soothed my soul and I kept hoping that deer and moose might come to the pond to drink where I could see them. The many ponds near me had their special character. Crocker Pond was the nearest one and it attracted a lot of visitors in the summer. I often went there just to see the way the water reflected the dark green pine trees. Crocker Pond had a very distinctive granite rock that protruded out of the water like the body of a whale.

Many ponds in Maine are called: Round Pond. The one I got to know was about a mile in the woods on a very buggy trail that led from Crocker Pond. It was ringed by green mountains and always perfectly still except for frogs jumping in and out of the water and fish coming up for air. It was always deserted and I think I was the only person that knew about it.

Broken Bridge Pond was also near Crocker Pond and was reached by a steep descent on a footpath. At dusk, there were lots of ducks honking back and forth. I would see fresh moose tracks around the pond. The view from the top of the trail to the pond was magnificent and sparkling in the setting sun. Another area, the Patte Brook Marsh, attracted a lot of water birds including graceful gray herons that balanced on one leg as if in a yoga class.

One summer evening, I went with my friend, Peter and his young daughter, Aurora, to Twitchell Pond. The shore of this small pond is dotted with huge boulders and towering cliffs where hawks dwell and squawk. There was a narrow sandy beach and from there we could gently glide our bodies into the middle of beds of pink water lilies and soak in the warm water.

I had a strange delight in the company of frogs—both the slimy ones around the ponds and the dryer ones that abounded in the forest. Some of them were tiny miniatures as small as my thumbnail. I often picked them up and actually remembered the old adage about kissing a frog and how it was supposed to turn into a handsome prince. I didn't really do that because I didn't believe this would happen. The frogs were fun anyway even though they pissed on my hands.

Midsummer was filled with long days that faded into ethereal twilight and then slowly into the night. Often the nights were swathed with thick layers of ground fog as the clouds seemed to come to the earth. When I drove through ground fog, it was like trying to drive through marshmallow fluff. In my bed, as I heard the birds sing their lullabies to each other, I fell into sleep so smoothly. Each night, I gazed up at the stars which were so brilliant here mixed in with dancing fireflies.

By August, I was able to enjoy eating lots of squash, lettuce and tomatoes from my garden. Many tomatoes did not ripen completely and I cooked lots of fried green tomatoes with garlic and onions. I always had a surplus of squash and I couldn't really eat it any more. Giving them away was quite an undertaking here that had to be done with some strategy. I took my extra squash to church and gave them to people I knew personally at the coffee hour after the service to make sure they had a good home.

As the apples had begun to turn red and ready for picking, the temperature became cooler. When I picked up my mail at the post office, people were talking about the inevitable night of the first frost. Blankets and quilts would be lovingly placed over tomato plants to protect them from damage. When the frost struck, the huge leaves on the squash plants shriveled overnight into the floppy black wings of monster bats.

By late August, the lily stalks had dried into hollow reeds. The hummingbirds had gone elsewhere. Soft lavender asters took over from the earlier blooming daisies. Milkweed pods were full grown and bursting their silky seeds into the crisper air where they would float gracefully on the wind. I picked all the berries I could find and the birds and the bears got the rest. Summer had exhausted itself in its ravishing dance, with bees, bugs and intensive growing. I soaked up as long as possible its splendor and especially the softness of the forest at dusk when little patches of leaves were backlit to an intense green as the sun moved beyond the horizon. Summer was leaving center stage and fall waited in the wings with its own act.

Reflections in the Brook

Chapter 10
Fall: Colored Splendor to Bareness

When the drama of fall began around my schoolhouse, I enjoyed an inspired performance of the energetic rhapsody of the leaves dancing wildly. The music of the colors played loudly all around me with an orchestra of trees. Being alone in the solitude of the forest, I was immersed in the finale of fantastic foliage. The whole landscape was transformed as the leaves changed from green to colors of lavish brilliance. Florescent streaks of hot color swirled through the crisp fall sky in a last glorious dance that dazzled my eye. I was living in an electric paint box. Colors more brilliant than the ones I could squeeze from my tubes of watercolor or mix with my pencils sailed past me in sparkling and shimmering intensity.

The air was chillier now and punctuated with the smell of wood smoke as it was the time to start burning wood to keep warm. The days shortened as the frost touched all plants and trees with its icy fingers. As October approached, the leaves on the maples were transformed into pulsing beings of orange and magenta majesty. The small, round poplar leaves turned to gold and spiraled downward in a shower of shining coins. The oak trees were the last to let go of their leaves that stayed a sedate brown. The mountainsides blazed with the colors of fire. Only the evergreens stayed calm in their year-long garb of dark green needles.

The big black snake that I often saw on the sunny ledge was underneath the schoolhouse, neatly coiled into a circle and hibernating already. The squirrels and chipmunks were very busy with their endless activity of laying in food for the winter. I could hear the chipmunks moving stuff under the house. The squirrels were racing back and forth digging up the land as they buried acorns. I could never understand how a squirrel could remember where all the nuts were. It was a kind of mystery. I myself had a lot of problems remembering where I left my car keys. It may be that squirrels would bury nuts in so many places that a hit and miss approach worked for them when it came to locating them when they were hungry.

In fall there was a spring in my step as the leaves on the ground became dry and crunchy. I became a serious leaf dancer and kicked up huge globs of leaves when I walked about the forest and did a few ballet jumps and turns. I loved dancing in the leaves that seemed to dance with me. Leaves became tiny boats when they landed on the surface of the brook and sailed gently downstream. The leaves fell rapidly, helped by heavy rains. Then suddenly, around mid October, all the trees were bare and there was a foot-high carpet of richly colored leaves throughout the forest.

The temperature slid down towards freezing. It was now time to get seriously organized for the winter. While I could still drive on the road before it would be blocked with snow, I brought in heavy things like lamp oil, pasta and bird seed so I would not have to backpack them in the winter. I cleaned up my garden and put it to bed for the winter. I pulled up the spent squash and tomato vines. I remembered to plant a bunch of garlic bulbs which were like tulips and had to be planted in the fall in order to bloom in the spring. I was able to salvage my many green tomatoes by individually wrapping them in newspaper. I put them inside in a cardboard box so they could ripen to red indoors. It seemed to work. I harvested rosemary, basil and dill and hung them up inside the schoolhouse to dry. The inside of the schoolhouse was rich with the fragrance of drying herbs.

Ripe Apples Ready to Drop

Fall was the time for picking apples from the many orchards nearby. I bought a whole bushel of apples from a nearby orchard. They were too many for me to eat before they would spoil. I cut them into thin round slices which I strung up on strings and hung inside the schoolhouse near the ceiling where I knew the mice couldn't reach. The apples dried in about a month. I liked the look of the long lines of apple circles hanging from the ceiling of my schoolhouse. I had a big supply of sweet dried apples that lasted well into the spring. I also dried meat and carrots. The process of drying food and herbs was to me a reminder of the way things might have been in an earlier time. I preserved food safely without using the electricity that refrigeration required and which I didn't have. It emphasized my feeling of going back in time.

A focus of activity in the fall was to make sure I would be warm in the winter. Getting lots of firewood and stacking it in convenient places took a lot of my time and physical energy. I had two cords of wood delivered in early September. I naively let the wood seller dump the wood on the side of the road. This was actually the only place he could dump it since there was no way he could drive his truck closer to the schoolhouse. I had no idea it would take me almost the entire day to stack it in an orderly manner. I did not have a clear sense of how big a cord of wood really was. It was long hard work. I wished someone would just magically materialize and help me, but not even a car came by. A chipmunk showed up to stare at me. He had a huge pine cone in his mouth. He stared at me so long I wondered if the pine cone was permanently stuck in his jaw, but at last he took it out of his mouth with his tiny paws and proceeded to delicately munch it. I was jealous because I could not eat pine cones like a chipmunk.

Stacking the wood went on and on. There was an endless mountain of big seventeen-inch chunks of heavy and not so dry hardwood. My only great consolation was that it was a Saturday and the Metropolitan Opera was coming in loud and clear, live on my portable radio. It was an obscure opera, *La Wally*, one that is almost never performed. I enjoyed it tremendously and sang along. I had not known just how much space three cords of wood would take up.

There was barely space for cars to get by on the narrow road. I knew that I had to move all this wood off the road before I went to bed otherwise some pickup truck might crash into it. I persisted as night approached consoled by knowing I would feel real comfortable in winter with all this wood stashed nearby and dry. The stars came out as I stacked the last logs. My muscles were sore for days, but I felt good because I had a sufficient supply of wood. While the road was passable, I also hauled in lots of scraps of hardwood from the Bethel Furniture Company about eight miles away on Route 2. These were free and very dry and were great for kindling. Heat was not going to be a problem here as long as I had a few matches.

Lines of Canadian geese flying in "v" formation stretched across the sky as they migrated to the south for the coming winter. They seemed to know where they were going, guided by internal radar. They make quite a clatter as they flew low over me and with their squawking and honking they sounded like barking puppies.

The deer were smart and started hiding—for good reason since hunting season was approaching. In October, the sharp sound of rifle shots began to shatter the tranquility of my peaceful forest. Orange-garbed hunters walked by the road carrying long rifles and looking for deer, moose and bear. There were three categories of the hunting season here. September was bow and arrow season and no guns were allowed. October was bear season and November was the busiest time because it was open season on deer. This made me fearful of walking around the forest as I should have wanted. I was afraid of being a target because I knew there were lots of hunters out there ready to shoot something that moved. I was sure they were even on my land despite my posting of "No Hunting" signs along the edges of my land. The signs had not been respected and I had seen them ripped off and on the ground. When I did go out, I wore bright orange so as to be as noticeable as possible. I did not want to be mistaken for an animal and shot at.

One day in October, I saw a dog wandering along the road with a beeper on its collar that was used to guide the hunters to deer or bear. In the comfort of their vehicle, the hunters could rotate an antenna and locate exactly the prey that the dog had found. Later as I further walked on the road, I came to a stopped pickup truck carrying a dead black bear. Looking at the bear close up, I was amazed at its size. It was fearsome and bigger than any human I had seen—and it had lived near me. Strangely I was never afraid of bears when we shared the forest and we were both in our natural habitat and kind of kin to each other.

I had never seen a dead bear. I was moved to touch its bristly black fur above its eyes. It felt like an overgrown crew cut. It was a very handsome animal. Part of me felt sad and I just wished that the hunters could leave these animals alone. Yet I also knew from talking to hunters that some of them greatly depended on hunting for their food. They could freeze the meat and it would last their family a long time. It was a way that humans could survive times of low employment. And in this sense, hunting was not just a sport. The Bureau of Land Management permitted the hunting seasons because it was a way of managing the numbers of the wildlife population. I knew this was necessary because I had personally seen deer killed by speeding trains right outside of Washington, D.C. where they were overpopulating an urban area.

In late fall, the rain touched the earth and it turned to ice. The path to the brook could became slippery. I nailed short pieces of rope to the gangplank that connected the deck to the schoolhouse to make it less slippery. It was almost too cold now in November to enjoy working outside, especially since the hunters kept me out of the forest. I turned my attention to cooking more elaborately and doing art. I made all kinds of soup automatically by just letting a pot simmer on top of the wood stove which I used every day. I began to slow down and sit around the stove more in my rocking chair, putting my inspiration into concrete form by painting and drawing, reading, and just being here now.

The days slowly shortened as night came earlier little by little. By early December, I was lighting the oil lamps around three thirty in the afternoon. As it got dark earlier, I often had to make an effort to stay awake. I did not want to totally hibernate like the bears. It would have been real easy to slip into my sleeping bags right after dinner and dream forever here. I was a bookworm and had so many books to read and letters to write to friends. I still mainly used candles and oil lamps, but by now I had bought two solar lanterns which became handy sources of free light. These lanterns had renewable photovoltaic cells and did not waste batteries or oil. In the morning I would place them outside in bright sunlight to recharge themselves sufficiently to run for a few hours. I liked solar energy because it was renewable and clean. I hoped that more and more people would turn to the use of solar power for their light and electricity and there would be less pollution and less dependence on gas and oil.

Electric light would have been a real intrusion into the chiaroscuro mood of the schoolhouse. The pure moonlight so often amazed me as it could light up the outdoors so finely. Even indoors, I was able to read just by the light of the moon. Moonlight had a special, magical quality of a different time in which the tones of reality were reversed as in a black and white negative. Moonlight here was so bright because it was completely uncontaminated by electric lights. I even dared to drive by pure moonlight alone on the back roads when I knew that there was no one else about. I would turn off my headlights and drive slowly on the familiar road. Without the headlights, as my eyes adjusted to the darkness, I could still see enough by moonlight and even see the shapes of the mountains looming in the distance.

I knew that the snow would be here soon. On a late November morning, I awoke to a scene of exquisite beauty. Overnight in total silence, the first snow had fallen and totally transformed the forest into shades of white. Every twig, every pine and fir needle, every dried weed was heaped thickly with the pure whiteness of the this first snowfall. Of course, one of my worst fears was realized. My car was still parked right across the road from the schoolhouse. I was worried that it could be stuck here until spring with what seems like four inches of snow on the ground. I decided to try and get the car out to the end of the plowed road as soon as possible—just in case there was more snow. Luck was with me and I did drive out. I stayed in the ruts made by some giant pickup trucks, and by accelerating greatly, I managed to get up the hill and miraculously reached the safe place to park. Now I knew that I had to start parking my car here at the school bus turnaround on the paved road and start walking in and out in the snow until the road would again be passable around May. I couldn't take the chance of getting my car snowed in and trapped on the unplowed road.

In early December, after the hunters left, I took long walks and discovered more easily the shape of the land and its dips and hills now more visible since the leaves were off the trees. There was a place of huge boulders that look as if they had been placed here as stepping stones for a giant. I also found a puddle about twenty feet wide and fantasized that this could be my own private skating rink in the winter with just enough space to jump and spin. Without the color of a canopy of leaves, the forest had a new, almost monochromatic appearance as a subtle composition of black, white, the dark green needles of the evergreens, and many shades of gray. The bareness of the trees made the varied textures of their bark more obvious. My hands caressed the smoothness and dazzling whiteness of the birch trunks with peeling thin layers of paper on its bark. I admired the ballet-like balance of trees and their outstretched branches gracefully extended into the sky. The trees remained alive, silent and strong. I could scratch a bare twig and always find the green that covered the stored energy for spring. The naked trees around my schoolhouse now revealed bird nests and, up higher, larger establishments for the squirrels. I had more than enough delight here to feed my senses and my soul with this beauty and wonder. Fall had begun in a flash of color and now moved towards the total stillness of winter and the continuing drama of the seasons.

Chapter 11
Stone Walls and Cellar Holes

Wood structures like the cabins of the early settlers and massive barns could burn and rot and disappear without a trace, but stone walls could last for many centuries. New England forests are crisscrossed with long runs of these old stone walls used to keep animals in a pasture and deer out of planted fields. As I tramped through the forest, I would encounter the stone walls which were often somewhat hidden like a half-buried treasure. Other leftover structures from the past were cellar holes. The voracious growth of the forest could swallow up the old cellar holes that once supported wooden houses. The forest around my schoolhouse held these sturdy traces of its history of long ago. I was fascinated with their strong presence and they made me feel connected to those people who built them and lived here in Mud City when it was a vibrant farming community a hundred years ago. I was amazed at how stones persisted despite the rough efforts of the freeze-thaw cycle common to Maine and the aggressive growth of trees, shrubs and plants in any crevice where soil developed. Despite crumbling and pushing from invading roots, the stone walls and cellar holes remain both as ruins and as a monument to the hard work involved in building them.

Stone Wall Along the Mud City Road

In spring when at last the thick snow melted, old paths and roads began to emerge slowly like a black and white print in a tray of developing solution. The Mud City Road, which had not been used be any vehicle in a very long time, was bordered by an old stone wall that I got to know very well. As I touched the old stone wall, I felt I touched the past. The construction of this type of wall was very simple and did not require cutting the stones nor the skill of a stone mason. Neither tools nor mortar were used; just the hard labor of lifting and positioning the stones in place. The stones were securely stacked on top of one another in layers and the weight of the layers kept them in place. The walls rose gradually as farmers cleared the land for growing and grazing by removing stones so their horse and oxen drawn plows could freely till the earth. The general structure was set with large stones and smaller ones were used to fill in and balance the larger stones. The walls were about two feet wide and never got more than about thirty inches in height. It would have been much harder to lift the stones higher and support a taller wall. Their low profile and use of local stone right out of the forest made them an integral part of the landscape.

The stone wall in my forest was sturdy despite beginning to become overgrown with young trees growing out of its sides. Its weather-worn stones were covered with thick layers of pine needles, bright green patches of moss and circular patches of lichens. The small crevices between the stones formed perfect vacation homes for the ground-dwelling chipmunks who often darted in and out. Often as I passed the wall in the good weather, I would clean out some of the accumulated dirt and vegetation because I wanted to keep this treasured wall as sturdy as possible. It seemed so full of memories and I almost expected the stones to talk. I followed the path of this wall and many others in the area and imagined when cows, sheep and horses had been grazing in the meadows the walls defined.

Before the lush forest growth almost hid it in June, I could also see a big cellar hole which was all that remained of a farm house that burned down long ago. I was told this was a two-story house, and part of a homestead that included a large barn, fields, orchards and cows. There was supposed to be a well nearby but I never found any trace of it. This cellar hole was made of enormous blocks of granite and had been built to last. The cellar was a most important part of a New England home for the early settlers. It was cool in the summer and warm in the winter because it was below the frost line. It was used to store food and keep it fresh. A corner of the cellar would often be filled with clean sand to make a root cellar. Vegetables such as turnips, parsnips, carrots and beets would be dug out of the gardens as winter approached and buried in the sand of the root cellar where they would stay fresh and not dry out. Because it could not freeze deep in the cellar, this was an ideal place to store food that had been canned in glass jars such as pickles, tomatoes, and jelly made from summer fruits.

The area around the cellar hole had once been cleared, but by now thousands of maple saplings were beginning to take over. The cellar hole was about twenty feet square and about seven feet deep and had shiny, silver birch trees growing out of its sides. There was a set of granite steps that ran down into its depth which was decreasing year by year with the accumulation of layers of leaves and pine needles. I thought of this cellar hole as a sunken garden that was taking on a new life of its own in the plan of nature. I would often linger there imagining what life was like there when the house was occupied. I pictured long leisurely summer afternoon lunches outside in the green splendor of the forest. Children would be running around the yard and in the nearby apple orchard playing games of tag and hide and seek. I could see faint rock outlines of garden areas where I knew irises and lilies had flourished. I wondered about the tragedy of the fire and if people had perished in the blaze and if the cellar hole had been a tomb. I hoped this was not the case.

Near the cellar hope were faint traces of the foundation for the big barn. I took to literally digging into the past and this once busy farmyard was my own private archeological dig. I would often scrape in the dirt there and find bits and pieces of artifacts such as an old left boot, about a women's size six, with nails all neatly cobbled around its thick leather sole, old bottles with their glass turned to iridescence, parts of carpentry tools, many horseshoes, as well as many pieces of broken crockery.

I continued exploring the land and tried to find a hidden spring that I had been told was nearby. One day, the former owner of the schoolhouse came by to visit and showed me exactly where it was. After a very short walk across my property line into what is technically known as the White Mountain National Forest land, we found the spring surrounded by lush trees and covered with some rotting boards and old leaves. I expected something more dramatic, but the spring was just a big hole in the ground that stayed filled with the best water I ever tasted. One day, as I scooped my hands like a cup into the fresh water and was drinking right out of the spring, I noticed something funny looking in the water. I reached my hand in and pulled it out. In horror and disgust, I realized it was a dead chipmunk. The water had tasted great and I did not get sick but I wasn't going to take any chances on having any more mammals drown in my drinking water. So I fished out all the rest of the debris like old branches and pine cones out of the spring and put a big piece of sheet metal over it with a big rock on top as a secure cover.

On humid oppressively hot days in midsummer, the water from this spring was sweeter than champagne. At one time, when the schoolhouse had been used as a hunting camp, the water from this spring used to flow into the schoolhouse through a hose laid in the brook. This eventually got chewed up by porcupines. If I had repaired the hose, I would have been able to pump water again into the sink in the schoolhouse. However, my reality was that I didn't need more than a bucket of water a day for cooking and washing which I could easily fetch from the brook. I did not have a lot of motivation for reconnecting the spring to the schoolhouse. I decided to keep things as simple as possible; besides, there was also no way I could change the gnawing habits of the porcupines.

These scattered traces of past human activity, like the stone walls and cellar hole, helped me imagine a time uncluttered by television, junk mail, traffic gridlock and consumerism. I had gone back to what seemed to me like a simpler time. I imagined neat rows of jars of homemade jam lined up on shelves in the cellar. I could almost hear the clatter of horses hooves as they cantered by the stone wall. I could smell the vinegar scent of apples lying on the ground around the old orchard in early fall. The memory of the people who lived here before me helped me feel less lonely because I imagined their presence and knew that they too had enjoyed this beautiful forest.

Chapter 12
A Tropical Interlude

It was hard to believe, but one winter I did really wind up on a warm and sunny island in the Caribbean for three weeks. One cold day in January, I got a letter from some friends from Boston who wanted to send me to St. Thomas in the Virgin Islands where their vacation home had suffered a lot of damage from a hurricane and other causes. The house needed a lot of skilled attention. My friends needed to get the house fixed up and thought I was the right person for the job. I agreed. I was given a round-trip plane ticket, lots of money and their credit card and told that a rental car would be waiting for me at the airport. It was an offer too good to refuse even though I was getting really dug into the comforting cocoon of my old schoolhouse tethered close to the warmth of the wood stove. The thought of lying on a sandy beach and an all-expenses-paid trip was very compelling. I was tired of wearing so many layers of clothing here in the thick of winter. I could come back with a tan and make everyone jealous.

I loaded all the carpentry tools I could fit into a huge suitcase and headed to Logan Airport in Boston. Although I loved the beauty of winter, I was fantastically glad to be leaving all the cold, snow and ice thousands of miles behind. I also looked forward to the challenge of doing the work. I loved doing carpentry and had a lot of experience in home repair. Wood was in my blood since my father was a cabinetmaker and five of my brothers also worked in that field. I liked the aspect of bringing order and beauty out of chaos as I repaired things.

After three progressively smaller flights—to Miami, to San Juan, and then to St. Thomas—I and my tools were in another, very warm world. I still had on thermal underwear suitable for New England weather so I ducked into a ladies' room and peeled off my layers of clothing to a comfortable t-shirt and shorts I had worn underneath everything. Like clockwork, my rental car was waiting for me. I was a little apprehensive about driving on the left-hand side of the road with a car that had a steering wheel on the right-hand side. Making turns seemed all wrong and scary, but I seemed to have adjusted OK. I followed the map I had been given and soon arrived at my friends' empty house without any accidents. And, of course, I just basked in the warm sun of this tropical paradise.

As soon as I saw their house, it was clear that my work was cut out for me. Like my schoolhouse in Maine, this house in St. Thomas needed tons of tender loving care. My friends' house was high on a hill and I admired a magnificent view of the sparkling water of Frenchman's Bay below. I walked down the stairs past an overgrown yard and flown off shingles to the front entrance with boards that had been chewed up and pulled loose by the previous renter's dogs. The inside of the house was filled with trash, dirty and in great disarray. Cabinet doors off their hinges, chipped paint, loose door knobs and other broken things greeted me. There were two bedrooms, a living room and a huge deck looking out to the water. All this was calling to me to clean, organize and make it beautiful again. I switched into my creative handywoman mode. My compulsive fixer-upper instinct was aroused and active. The first thing I did was to document the condition of the house. I took out my camera and made a series of "before" photos which I would use to contrast with the "after" photos.

I made a thorough inspection of the place, listed, planned and sequenced the work. Finally I cleaned out a place to sleep and rested for the next day's adventures in good housekeeping.

This experience of being sent to a tropical paradise was not completely new to me. A few years earlier I had been sent to Hawaii on a similar mission. While most people could only afford to go there on vacation or in their dreams, I was able to live in on the island of Oahu free for three months in exchange for doing a lot of repairs on a house owned by the parents of a friend of mine. I had many opportunities to experience the beauty of the mountains, foliage and endless beaches. Here, in the Virgin Islands, I would have similar opportunities. It was amazing how my life bumps me into places of outstanding natural beauty that I would never have thought of visiting.

The next day, I woke up refreshed and plunged into the work with a furious energy. It was exhausting and yet very satisfying to see the inside of the house become habitable, less chaotic and more beautiful. I started by sweeping the floors and when I moved the bed I had slept in the previous night, I saw a monstrous furry spider the size of a substantial cantaloupe crouched behind it. This spider was worse than any of the mice and bats I had encountered in the schoolhouse. My skin cringed all over and I was afraid of what I think was a monster tarantula. My friends did not tell me they had a pet spider nor about the scorpions which I also encountered here and there underneath things as I was cleaning up. Maybe I would not have come if I knew. Big bugs are my tragic flaw but I was glad the spider did not have wings. He relocated elsewhere—outside the house when I was able to sweep him out with a fast broom.

In St. Thomas, the weather was always warm, very pleasant with not one rainy day. I enjoyed this but did not think I would want to live here year round since I needed the rhythm and contrasts of the seasons in New England. Too much good weather would be boring. The afternoons could get extremely hot. Since it was too hot for working outside, I got into the good habit of taking a siesta until around four when it started to cool and then working with renewed energy until eight. I soon patched and painted the walls in the house. The house was a lot cleaner now and I began to enjoy the patterns of light and shadow from the louvered windows. I got used to the house and ate my meals on the deck drinking in the views of the water and the so-warm sunshine and extravagant sunsets of gold and pink.

I soon explored the immediate neighborhood heavy with flowering magenta bougainvillea, hibiscus and palm trees and found that I was within very easy walking distance of the Limetree Resort. It cost more money to stay there than I would ever imagine paying. I was glad I could just stay in my friends' house for nothing. There was a bar and a disco in the resort which really did not interest me. I was able to easily sneak into the resort's pool. Lying on my back in the water staring up at the sky fringed with palm trees felt so good after the exhaustion of hard physical labor. For the first time in my life I also worked up my courage to jump into the deep end of the pool. I overcame my fear of sinking and I knew my body was naturally buoyant and would just rise up to the surface with plenty of time to breathe.

At night, I was really tired. I wound down by curling up with Jack London's *Stories for Boys*, a good book that was lying around the house. I read it and wondered if there was something specifically masculine about these tales of adventure in the cold northwest that I, as a woman, would not perceive. The stories were an enjoyable link to my home in the cold northeast, in my old schoolhouse in Maine where it was raging winter and extremely cold. I could easily imagine the snow drifting higher and higher around the schoolhouse. What a difference latitude makes in climate!

I was glad I took siestas. The afternoons were quieter than the nights when sleeping was often difficult because there was a lot of noise here in St. Thomas. Watch dogs, especially, would howl all night as they protected their territory from intruders. One dog would start a solo howl and soon all the other dogs from near and far would join in for hours. Sleeping at night was not easy in paradise, since I was not a night owl like the tourists and locals seemed to be. The disco music at Limetree pounded through the hot night air. Bugs kept finding my skin very tasty and kept biting endlessly. Then, there was always one mosquito that was determined to tunnel into my ear and would keep buzzing around me. I was also afraid that monster spider would return with buddies.

The island of St. Thomas was a popular destination for cruise ships. From the deck high on the hill, I watched the brightly lit-up cruise ships, that looked like huge sparkling snails, as they slowly oozed into the harbor. Tourists flooded the streets of the port of Charlotte-Amalie and spent lots of money making tourism the mainstay of the local economy. Popular tourist attractions, such as the castle of the notorious pirate Bluebeard, evoked the history and legends of seafaring brigands who once roamed the Caribbean. As a non-tourist, I was able to see another facet of the character of the island as I roamed away from the flashy tourist places and saw areas of outright poverty in the hills that reminded me of the impoverished Nicaraguan countryside.

I naturally wanted to see and experience everything I could while I was here. There were many other islands nearby—including St. Johns, Tortola, and St. Barts. When I felt I had made good progress on my friends' house, I decided to become a tourist myself and went on a day cruise to visit these other islands. They were beautiful gems surrounded by smooth sand in a sparkling blue sea. I pounced on the clean beaches and delighted as the waves creeped up and over my feet and tickled my toes. On the cruise, I had the opportunity to try snorkeling. I failed at this because the mask made me uncomfortably claustrophobic and I could not wear it. All was not in vain as I had on a floatation vest and was able to feel very comfortable in the water as I slowly paddled around the anchored ship. I did not wear goggles on my eyes and I kept ducking my head under the salty sea and opening my eyes. I was rewarded with a vision of an amazing array of brightly colored white fish with stripes of blue and yellow swimming all around me.

During my three-week stay on the island, I took the ferry from Red Hook Harbor on St. Thomas to St. Johns Island a number of times. Here I sensed a very different mood from the hustle and bustle of St.

Thomas. There were less people here and more green space. The interior of St. Johns was filled with wild emerald mountains and there were very few houses. Most of St. Johns was a national park with endless trails through the jungle and along the shore. Even in the heat, I could feel comfortable walking because of the sea breeze and the shade. I walked in so much beauty here and there were hardly any other hikers around to destroy my solitude.

One afternoon, on St. Johns, I climbed Peace Hill where there was an old windmill surrounded by a huge stand of organ pipe cactus. Nearby, there was a statue of Christ of the Caribbean depicted as a megalith with no facial features, powerful just by its size. I sat there quietly as around me the sea shimmered in colors of turquoise and jade. Soon my meditative state on this hill was interrupted by the arrival of a pair of very garish-looking tourists. The man was wearing orange swimming trunks and a beanie with a propeller spinning on the top of his head from the breeze. The woman was wearing a plaid bikini with high heels. Inside I yelled, "ouch" to myself in protest at their outlandish garb which clashed next to the fully clothed statue. I was sure they were from central casting as stereotypes of tourists. This fashion intrusion was a kind of reality check and a message that I would never get too comfortable with this place.

I continued walking along those wonderful trails and the extravagant tropical vegetation reminded me of what I had seen in Hawaii. The diversity of the trees with their giant leaves made me feel like a minor character in a primitive painting by Henri Rousseau dwarfed by bay rum trees, strangler figs, wild antheriums, and kapok trees with their huge buttressed roots rising almost six feet off the jungle floor. When I got tired of walking, I found the road and hitched a ride back to the ferry at Cruz Bay past wild donkeys and goats and soon returned to St. Thomas.

I kept working hard on my friends' house. With the interior under control, I was now able to pay attention to the outside. I replaced the trim boards the former tenants' dogs had chewed up. I was lucky because I had brought all the tools I needed, including some power tools. I got a load of cinder blocks delivered and made a low wall at the top of the road above the house to keep rain water from running down into the house. I made a border of gravel around the perimeter of the house which would keep weeds from growing there and provide decent drainage. I positioned some of the cinder blocks on the hill to control the erosion. It was hard, hot and sweaty work but I enjoyed it.

My hands were sore and rough from the concrete work. Soon I cleared some rocks and debris off the front hill. I purchased a few ponytail palms and a bunch of cactus plants from a nursery on the other side of the island. These could also control the erosion on the downward slope to the house. With a little landscaping, the place began to look better. The cactus plants were studded with needles and had to be handled very carefully. Luckily I had my ski gloves with me and they saved my hands from further abuse.

I was able to hire people to do the electrical work, replace the blown-off shingles and paint the roof from an expense account. I learned that it was very important to seal the roof well with rubber paint since the run-off was collected in below-the-ground cisterns and used by the occupants of the house for their water supply. There were no wells here although some of the more affluent residents had their own desalinization plants and could get their water from the sea.

It was all too soon time to fly north. On my last night here, it was so fitting to enjoy a jewel of a sunset. I sat on the newly painted deck overlooking Frenchman's Bay and watched the sky slowly shade from lavender to glowing orange with purple gray clouds so still and calm over the cobalt-silver shimmer of the sea. A chorus of chirping crickets provided the right musical accompaniment. The gold disk of the sun dropped down into the western sea. Then there came that magical moment when the sea and sky merged and became the same dark ink of night. I said an emotional farewell to this place I was privileged to visit. It was so different from the snow and total winter whiteness of my old schoolhouse in Maine. I marveled that I was even able to have been here at all because of the miracle of jet travel. I was thankful my friends had hired me to go here but eager to be back in the totally quiet solitude of my forest.

Chapter 13
Small Town Life and Visitors

I soon made connections with many people in the town of Bethel. As I lived alone in the schoolhouse, I had started talking to the little mouse that would keep showing up near my desk. He would poke his head out from the little hole he had in the wall. I called him Giorgio after an ex-boyfriend from Italy. I knew that I needed to be alone to deeply experience all the wonder in the forest that surrounded me and to do my creative work. I also knew that I would lose my sanity if I kept talking to mice.

Even without a phone I could keep busy with activities in town. I was pleasantly surprised to find out that there were a fair amount of things to do here. There was not the overwhelming quantity of choices that were available in the city, but just enough things focused around politics, the environment, and my church including dance school recitals and high school plays—and ticket prices were real reasonable. Even Bethel had its own spectacular performance of the Nutcracker Ballet produced by the director of the local dance school.

I wanted to learn about Bethel and soon became involved in the Bethel Area Task Force—an exciting diverse group of local residents committed to making Bethel a better place culturally and economically. I clearly felt a closeness to people here because of our common love for the abundance of natural beauty in the mountains, ponds, and trees.

Because the lifestyle here was different and distant from the racing and rushing of the city, people seemed more relaxed and had the time to enjoys friendships more. I especially enjoyed talking to people who had lived here all their lives even though I was aware that they would always consider me a "flatlander," that is, someone not from this very mountainous region. The different rhythm to life here focused around the seasons and included apple picking, harvesting corn, the fall foliage season which brought many leaf peepers, the ski season, and the summer visitors. After being in the area a few months, I could always count on seeing someone I knew at the post office when I picked up my mail. Because I lived so far in the woods, there was no mail delivery to my door. Picking up my mail in Bethel became a welcome social occasion for me and a lot of other people, especially in winter when the snow kept people more isolated.

The first people I made a point of visiting were the former owners of my schoolhouse. Jim and Flora Everett were an older couple who lived about eight miles down the road towards Route 2 in a small house, surrounded by bird feeders, next to an enormous barn. Flora had a heart condition that kept her almost bedridden but she delighted in the variety of birds that came to the feeders she had placed in her front yard. She spent many hours at her front picture window enjoying the views. Jim was often busy in the barn fixing things and keeping a flock of old trucks and tractors in running order. The Everetts had a lot of land in the area and were a gold mine of information about local people, places, and the cultures of hunting and logging. I visited them often and always enjoyed talking with them around their wood stove.

I was amazed to meet other people who lived well without electricity. I learned that I surely wasn't the only one living out of the range of the power grid. One family raised beautiful angora goats that were so soft to touch and had such curly fleece. They also had ducks.

They got their water in a gravity feed system from a hillside spring and this did not require any electricity for a pump since the water simply flowed downhill.

I attended the Congregational Church, also called "Congo" for short, in the center of town. In addition to the service, activities at the church included the choir, ladies' fellowship, and a wonderful coffee hour after the Sunday service. The ladies' fellowship held elegant, friendly luncheons which often featured many varieties of colorful, shimmying Jell-O mold. I remember one luncheon in particular which was held at a country inn with great mountain views and which was a goodbye party for a woman who was moving out of state to a retirement community. We savored an elegant meal and we all agreed that the food was presented in the style of "little old lady food." A dainty portion of chicken a la king on waffles and peach crisp was served garnished with bright orange puffy lantern flowers and johnny jump-ups. The woman who was leaving lasted two months away in Pennsylvania and came back to stay in Bethel where all her friends were because she missed them so much.

In December, the members of the Congo church organized the Holiday Fair. I helped make Christmas wreaths with fragrant balsam fir branches left over from logging activities. A highlight of the fair was a cookie walk. Many varieties of homemade cookies were arrayed on a decorated table. You forgot your diet, paid a fee and were given an empty, decorated coffee can. Then you had the mouth-watering privilege of walking around the table and putting as many of the dazzling and delicious cookie creations in your coffee can as would fit. The bakers in the church, including both the ministers, tried to outdo each other and show off their skills as they produced gingerbread, rich brownies, sugar cookies with green and red sprinkles, pfeffernuesse, and more.

One project that developed as a result of people putting their heads together on the Bethel Area Task Force was the "Just Imagine" Coffeehouse. As a singer, I loved being involved in presenting concerts and sharing music. The coffeehouse was always delightfully entertaining. It was held on Saturday nights in the good-sized and recently renovated basement of the Congregational Church in Bethel. It had the enthusiasm and support of the two ministers who were husband and wife and also avid musicians. I was part of a group that started it and I suggested the title to indicate that we were open to all kinds of musical possibilities. We wanted to create more performing opportunities for local musicians and places to have fun that were not in bars. While folk music with guitars and vocals predominated, it was not unusual to also enjoy yodelers, fiddlers, classical musicians and spontaneous dancing. This was a great and friendly place to be on a Saturday evening and the music would go on until near midnight. Our audience included people of all ages and especially families with children.

I became involved in local politics early on and helped a friend who was running for state representative go door-to-door in parts of the district. Later, I became active in a campaign for health care reform. A lot of residents closer to my schoolhouse in Albany were very concerned about a proposal to build a gambling casino on some land that was owned by the Passamoquoddy Indian Tribe. This was defeated after a lot of fiery debate in Albany Town Hall during which it became clear that the people who were really going to build the casino and make the most money were not Native American at all. Many people also felt that it would endanger the beauty of the area. I don't think that the casino has ever been built there.

In a small town, such as Bethel, tragedies seemed to hit harder and have more impact because more people were related or knew each other. The disasters were not just headlines in the paper. One winter a local family experienced a horrible loss as their new home burned to the ground from a fire caused by a wood stove. The family whom I knew from the church was not in their house at the time and no one was injured. They had just finished the long hard work of building their new home and they quickly lost everything.

One weekday I noticed that the streets in Bethel were clogged with Maine state troopers as they attended the funeral of another state trooper and his wife who had died as their small plane crashed into Mt. Will, right outside of the town. The couple's daughter, who was about twelve, had miraculously escaped unhurt and was able to walk off the mountain in the night and get help. This was an amazing feat since she could have fallen easily. I had often hiked up that same mountain in daylight and I knew that it had many, dangerous, steep ledges.

In the summers I took my carpentry tools and joined with a lot of others from my church as we worked on week-long house raisings for some families who needed their own homes. We worked with a local social service agency and the homes were completed in a few weeks. It was a lot like working with Habitat for Humanity which I had done in Boston and Nicaragua. I did a lot of framing with two-by-six timbers for the structure of the walls. Later I worked on adjusting and nailing the roof trusses in place. Banging nails felt good and natural even though it was very hot in the intense summer sun. We stayed at a church in the nearby town of Norway and had great meals prepared by church members there, including casseroles and more Jell-O molds.

In winter it was harder to get around as the snow piled up higher and higher. I mainly hibernated in the very comfortable cocoon of my schoolhouse. Since I knew a lot of people in town, I would occasionally get a house-sitting position for a few days. In exchange for making sure that the heat stayed on and the pipes did not freeze, I had a chance to luxuriate in a place with hot water, a bathtub, a TV, and perhaps, a piano. I fed the wood stoves, cats, dogs and goldfish, if necessary.

The possibility of free downhill skiing was very tempting. I lived about twelve miles from the Sunday River Ski Area which had a policy of not checking for lift tickets until nine on weekday mornings. It was possible and OK to ski the first hour free if I could get there at eight when the ski lifts started operating. For a short time, I became an early bird and managed to do a little downhill skiing for free. In order to make a quick escape to the ski slope, I would sleep in my ski clothes and walk out a mile on the snow-clogged road to my car which I had to park a mile away at the last plowed place. I would drive to Sunday River, jump into my skis and catch the lift to the top of a trail where often I would be the first person. I took my time going down and traversed the slope with long zig-zagging, making the runs last as long as possible. However, the trails were often dangerously icy, especially if the snow had melted the previous day and froze overnight. There was no way for my skis to grip the snow since the trail had not yet been groomed. Once the trail was sheer ice and there was no way my skis would grip it. The only thing I could do was to sit down and slide down the mountain on the seat of my pants. Though not a dignified style, it was much safer that way.

Downhill skiing was exhilarating but too scary. I wondered about the sanity of this sport when I heard about the death of a skier who had lost control and went into the trees. It was a winter with very little snow and I felt that all the unnatural manmade snow and slick icy trails could have contributed to that. I soon decided to stay with cross-country skiing right around my schoolhouse where I had no commute as it seemed simpler and more sensible. I could not afford to buy a lift ticket and ski on the downhill trails when they were groomed and safer.

There were a lot more activities after mud season and in the summer. Vacationers would arrive in abundance to enjoy this most beautiful part of the state and to explore the White Mountains in nearby New Hampshire. There were many summer homes and country inns, some of which had been the large houses of citizens prominent in the history of Bethel. *Maine* Street led to the Bethel Common which was a grassy open area on a hill with benches surrounded by the public library, some bed and breakfasts, the Bethel Inn, and an antique shop. This area around the Common was designated as a national historic district because of the significance of the old buildings there. One of the well-maintained old homes was the Moses Mason House which had once belonged to a prominent local physician, businessman and politician. Today it serves as the office of the Bethel Historical Society and has a small museum. The grounds around the house had a white painted gazebo and were filled with apple trees and luxurious beds of flowering perennials. Peonies with their delicate fragrance abounded and I would just keep going back there to inhale their delicate fragrance. Huge purple globe thistles would bloom later in the summer looking like sparklers frozen in time. Women from the Bethel Garden Club volunteered their time and skills to maintain these gardens which always looked wonderful. They knew exactly how to keep the sequence of the various flowers blooming all through the summer.

Bethel's very unique community celebration was Mollyocket Day which took place during a July weekend. This very popular event celebrated the life of a local Indian princess who according to local legend had done many good deeds. Festivities included a big parade up Maine Street and a concert and games on the Bethel Common. I was asked to march in the parade as the Count, a character from Sesame Street that I was not familiar with. The provided costume was made of wool and felt and was like wearing a sauna. I was trapped inside and I could barely see through the two tiny eye holes in the mask. Despite feeling like fainting, I managed not only to march but to pass out candy and made it through the extent of the parade route. The kids I saw seemed to be delighted as I waved to them and counted out the numbers from one to ten. Later in the afternoon, I rented a frog and entered the frog-jumping contest. This was a completely new experience for me. I lost, of course. Those who won brought their own frogs who they had probably trained for months. In the pie-eating contest, competitors plunged their faces into gooey blueberry pies and had to eat with their hands behind their back. Local bands played music throughout the day and into the early evening as townspeople and many vacationers enjoyed themselves in the good summer weather. I also performed as a folk singer, accompanying myself on guitar.

One thing I enjoyed a lot in town was swimming at the Country Club at the Bethel Inn. My major splurge was for a membership there that let me use the pool anytime. There was a golf course but I wasn't interested in playing golf. The outdoor pool was open all year round and very nicely heated. Despite all my years of living, I had never yet learned to swim because I never really had the time to concentrate on doing it. I also had a fear of the water from when people tried to teach me to swim when I was a child and I had no idea about how to float. In a local secondhand store, I came across a *Sports Illustrated* book on how to swim. The step-by-step instructions looked very clear. I bought the book for fifty cents, read it, relaxed and followed its directions and taught myself how to swim. At last I began to feel very comfortable in the water, even the deep end. I found that it was impossible for me to sink. If I just dived in, I would soon float to the surface. I spent many wonderful hours in that pool. When I got tired of the physical exertion of swimming, I would just flip over and float on my back and stare at the clouds or stars and rest. My body loved the heated water of the pool and I could swim in the winter when it was snowing and even when it was twenty degrees below zero. When it was so cold that my hair would freeze, I would just duck back into the warm water. When it was snowing, I would float on my back and feel the snowflakes landing gently on my face one by one. I would swim in the rain with steam rising from the surface and raindrops forming pulsing circles all around me as I evolved into a fish, a frog and a water ballerina. There were also showers with lots of hot water at the pool that I found very handy since, of course, I had none at the schoolhouse where I took bucket baths to stay clean.

Besides the public library, the Bethel Inn lobby was also a most comfortable place to spend some time. I was not a guest but no one ever hassled me. I could sit on real furniture like soft stuffed chairs as I leisurely read newspapers and magazines often in front of the welcome warmth from a massive fireplace. Artworks hung on the papered walls. There was a grouping of original pen and ink drawings by Charles Dana Gibson, a famous illustrator whose distinctive drawings of women with upswept hair produced the Gibson Girl look which was emulated by many women in the early part of the 1900s. In one of the hallways off of the lobby, there was also an enclosed phone booth with a seat that was a comfortable place to make phone calls to keep in touch with my kids and friends from other states.

My out-of-state friends that visited me waited for the summer's good weather when they could drive all the way to the schoolhouse door. They were clearly on vacation and they wanted to have a good time. It seemed to me that they often didn't trust my cooking on the campfire outside my front door in summer. Therefore, they took me out to dinner in some of the many good restaurants in the area which I enjoyed. It was nice to know that I had some friends from out of state who were brave enough to venture up here and endure the bugs, no running water and the outhouse.

The Interior of the Schoolhouse

One day my friend Larry whom I had met in Mexico showed up by surprise. He had driven up all the way from Virginia and asked around town and found out where I lived. He showed up at a busy time when I was in the throes of building a bedroom out of the shed and had tools and wood scattered all around the interior of the schoolhouse. I did not really expect him at all. It was a real effort to switch gears and enjoy his company and to be decently sociable to someone who had driven such a great distance to Maine. Then again, I did not have a phone and I had not checked my mail in about a week. I was relieved when he said that he had decided to stay in a motel in town. So I did not have to orientate him about bathing in the brook or using ashes in the outhouse. Larry was a retired businessman and I did not think he would be comfortable roughing it, but he had a great sense of adventure and had done a lot of sailing in his life.

I graciously endured lots of suggestions for improving my life at the schoolhouse. Most visitors were from cities and wanted to tell me how I should do this or that to make life here more like city living with all its conveniences. They told me I needed to get electricity. I had adjusted well to living without electricity. I had once asked the power company how much it would cost to get electricity and was told that it would be at least five thousand dollars to bring in a line from a mile away. This was too much money to be worth it. I believed that power would be a distraction from the beauty around me. It was also suggested that I should get a well dug and a pump so I could have a flush toilet and running water inside the schoolhouse. I tried to explain that I actually liked getting my water from the brook and enjoyed the reflections of the trees on the water. I tried to understand that my friends meant well and were trying to be helpful. One friend thought that the two-by-six plank that I used as a bridge across the brook was too narrow and insisted I should make a wider bridge because someone could fall into the water. I thought to myself that it would be no big deal if someone gets wet and I fumed silently. I was perfectly content with my narrow plank that wobbled and bounced when I walked across it. The truth was I liked things the way they were: simple, maybe primitive, but functional.

To be honest, I often felt smothered when friends stayed a few days. My schoolhouse was set up for contemplation, solitude and hard work. It was like a hermitage. Alone, I had no necessity to be sociable and conversant. With another person there, my tranquility was disturbed. I felt my relaxed rhythm of living was interrupted by my desire to make sure my visitors had a good time. Still I did enjoy guests from time to time. I did not want to keep on talking to mice all the time.

Living in a small town was different for me but I adjusted to its slower pace. I loved being far away from the rat race of a big city. I enjoyed the town of Bethel and my friends there, but I was more drawn to deeply experiencing the solitude and splendor of the forest around my schoolhouse. Although I was only ten miles from Bethel, my location deep in the forest often seemed to me to be in a simpler world and the different time frame that I needed. I felt sustained by the endless beauty of the forest and the joy of creating artwork even though I was lonely at times and I had hope that I would one day share my art with others.

Chapter 14
Epilogue and Leaving

After much thought, I decided to leave Maine for good on my way to two years in Bolivia working as a Peace Corps volunteer in rural sanitation and the arts. As I lived in the schoolhouse, time had been comfortably suspended between the present and the past in the special time zone in the forest. Eventually there came to me a consciousness that I could not live here any longer. It was sad to leave the beautiful forest and surrounding mountains, but I could not continue to survive there artistically, socially and economically. I recognized that it was time to move on to other challenges. I had always wanted to join the Peace Corps and felt my skills would be valuable helping poor people have a better life.

Although my experience of the forest always continued to deeply move me with its constant drama, wildness, grace and grandeur, I knew I was not a hermit nor did I wish to evolve into an unintentional recluse. I had lived alone in the forest enough and I knew that I needed to keep up the search for deeper friendships and community. I was always ecstatic to be surrounded by all the artistic inspiration from the forest, but I still knew that I needed to be connected with the very kindred spirits of other artists and try to make and find more possibilities for an audience for my work. It was not possible for me to get a sense of how this connecting could happen in rural Maine. I had enjoyed being involved in community activities in Bethel and it was hard to leave the new friends I had made here. My decision to leave was finalized after the painful experience of being very badly robbed by someone I knew. This was made more painful and frustrating when I realized that the police and the county sheriff would not even question the person who robbed me.

So I reluctantly decided to put the schoolhouse on the market. It was sad to sell it but there was no way to keep it. It needed a new owner. I was very concerned about the ever-increasing problem of vandalism. Windows had been broken when people did not see my car and figured I was not around. I had seen signs of attempted break-ins, like chisel marks around a door frame and a door pried open. Beer bottles had been often thrown into my lily beds. I prayed that someone would buy the schoolhouse soon and really love it, protect it and enjoy the forest. I had put a lot of love, sweat, energy and imagination into my forest home. I had never felt like I was just doing physical work. It was always done in joy and had its own pleasure in the moment. I enjoyed the process of fixing up the schoolhouse and making it an attractive space that was truly my home.

Although I thought the schoolhouse looked great, it took a long time for it to be sold—mainly because of the "primitive" conditions, lack of conventional utilities like electricity and running water, and no access by vehicles in winter. Ironically, I had come to view these inconveniences as part of the daily rhythm of life and blessings to be savored as my life slowed down in the schoolhouse. I actually enjoyed the one mile walk through the snow in the peace of winter. It was a pleasure to get my water from the brook that never froze and the nearby crystal clear spring. I admired the warm glow of oil lamps which gave me enough light. My outhouse worked perfectly with no pipes to freeze. I even had become friends with the bats whom I loathed at first. It seemed that most people saw all these acquired pleasures of mine as too many problems that did not endear them to the schoolhouse. While I was trying to sell the schoolhouse, I was working in Bolivia and I worried about it so much. I was afraid someone might burn it down. I had many dreams about my home hidden in the forest and how its location was half forgotten and the roads became more and more overgrown. Eventually it did sell while I was still in Bolivia and that was very good news. I was relieved that the schoolhouse would now have someone new to take care of it.

After the Peace Corps, I returned to Boston and bought a small condominium. I was fortunately within easy walking distance of two very beautiful green places: the Arnold Arboretum which is nothing less than a large museum of thousands of varieties of trees from all over the world with wonderful paths and hills and Jamaica Pond with its ever-changing water surface and abundance of water birds. I drew on these places for their natural beauty that fed my hungry soul. I set up a studio and plunged into my creative work dipping into the deep filled well of inspiration from the culture and landscape of Bolivia as well as Maine. I still yearned to be back in Maine, in the wildness of the forest and on the Appalachian Trail where I could touch and see all shades of green in the profusion of trees, ferns, and moss and where one foot in front of the other slowly led me across cool brooks and up and down mountain tops. I needed to again see the stars shine brightly at night in the clear, undisturbed air.

In the July after I had resettled into Boston, I drove back to Maine and Mud City to hike again the Mahousuc Trail and to satisfy my curiosity about what the schoolhouse might look like now, almost four years since I had last seen it. Before hitting the trail, I camped overnight in one of the hidden meadows near the schoolhouse that I am sure only I knew about. It was the height of the growing season. Daisies and black-eyed Susans abounded as did the bugs. It felt so good to be back in Mud City and lie on my back at night and see the surrounding trees reaching into the starry sky. Once again, I woke up in the morning and washed my face in a nearby brook and heard only the sweet polyphony of the birds.

As I deeply breathed the fresh mountain air, I gathered up my courage and prepared for the changes I would surely see in the schoolhouse. I slowly drove by my former schoolhouse home. I was very surprised at the radical changes. It could have been a different schoolhouse somewhere else. The new owners had been very busy adding their own improvements. All the land around the schoolhouse had been cleared and was empty. There was even a lawn of grass, something that I would never have considered. There were fewer trees and no little baby trees, no lilac bushes and no berry bushes. I didn't see any of the many lovely perennials that Peter had given me. They seemed to have vanished or maybe they were bulldozed away. The big bunches of orange day lilies under the windows were also gone. I could only hope that they were planted somewhere else. My old schoolhouse now existed only in my memory and in the many photographs I had taken. I have accepted this change but not without some sadness because the schoolhouse represented so much peace of the rich green forest to me. I know that there are "different strokes for different folks" and was glad to see the new owner or owners had been doing things their own way here. I certainly had.

The new owners had installed a big propane tank next to the house so they could have a quick way to heat the place. To me its large rounded white presence looked like a jarring note but perhaps worth it for quick warmth. I saw that they had painted the schoolhouse bright white, replaced the old corrugated metal roof with a shiny green one and removed the black shutters I had installed. The new owners had added some wooden lawn ornaments like big wooden cutouts of butterflies and daisies. I understand that my taste was not their taste. So passes time, and life goes on as the chapter of my life in the schoolhouse had ended. As I have moved on with my own life, so did the schoolhouse. I noticed there were no other cars around and no one was about. This was just as well as I was feeling awkward about meeting the new owners and I could continue staring. I soon noticed a big fluffy cat sitting in a window. Right away I felt better thinking that if the new owners liked cats, they are real OK people.

There are many lessons from my schoolhouse that are always with me. I learned I am of the earth and need to be close to nature to live well. I have become more and more aware of the beauty and fragility of the work of art we live on, planet earth. What I learned was not from scientific explanations and other people's words but the direct and deep experience of so much wonder and uncountable details from snowflakes to light green fir tips, to golden sunset clouds as well as the whole picture.

I learned also that I could live simply and well in extreme cold without appliances, gadgets, and many disposable consumer goods. I didn't do this to prove anything, I just wanted to BE in the schoolhouse in the forest. I well know that so much of the world's population lives without running water, flush toilets, and electricity not by choice but by their circumstances. From my travels in Latin America, I have seen how poverty and bad housing led to much suffering and I have become so aware of how our world is severely threatened by pollution and over-consumption. Poverty from a scarcity of resources greatly contributes to diseases that shorten the lives of many, especially young children. Cholera kills many young children and it could be prevented if people had clean drinking water. Chagas disease is rampant in Bolivia because the insect that causes it lives in the straw roofs of the houses of poor people who can't afford a wood or metal roof. In Maine, I always had clean water to drink. In Bolivia, I realized how scarce water was when I saw women and girls walking great distances with jugs to find and carry back water for their families. Often the only water they could obtain there was polluted from human, animal and mining wastes to the point of being toxic. In the rich forest of Maine, I always had enough rain to water my garden. In Bolivia, the time of rain was becoming more and more uncertain and droughts and floods were ravaging the land, damaging crops and making food scarce. In Maine, I was surrounded by trees. In the part of Bolivia where I lived, trees were scarce. Goats and sheep grazed everywhere and new trees had a difficult time surviving. I have a sad and horrible memory of being in a remote village in Bolivia called Molle Punku where I could look all around me and see no trees at all—just dusty hills. Here I saw an older woman walking by, her small body was bent and dwarfed by an enormous load of brush she was carrying tied to her back. The brush was all people here could use for cooking fires because there were no trees left for firewood. People here did not have money to buy gas or other fuel. Now there was no choice but to chop up bushes and saplings. Maine's forests were full of mature trees for heat and wood. I deeply sensed the contrasts between the abundance of water and trees in Maine and the depletion and scarcity of necessary natural resources in many parts of Bolivia where people suffered greatly from poverty and disease.

My life in the schoolhouse had been a privileged love affair with the greenness, abundance and beauty around me. I seek to continue this love affair for the rest of my life as I try to protect and honor the earth wherever I live. I have tried to advocate for environmental justice and stop further destruction of the earth which happens more and more in my own neighborhood in the Boston area where I now live. In my artistic work of creating paintings and drawings, I aspire to show reverence and amazement at the wealth of wonder in nature. The forest is my true home and where I feel the strong presence of the great artist who created all things with love, imagination, and sublime design. I will always seek to walk slowly in beauty in the forests for adventure, peace, renewal and especially splendor and solitude.

Author's Bio

Adventure, beauty, rich images, music, a search for justice and a reverence for the earth are some of the many colored threads that have woven the rich tapestry that is the weaving in progress of the life of Maria Termini.

She has created colorful and joyful artworks in silkscreen, watercolor, collage, colored pencil drawing and mosaics in the continual expression of her visual imagination which is especially inspired by her experience of the wonder and solitude of nature. Her artworks have been widely exhibited and are in the collections of many non-profit organizations, as well as the Boston Public Library and the Fogg Museum.

She is the mother of grown twins and has followed her bliss to backpacking adventures to Europe and South America, a solo bus trip to Central America, serendipitous carpentry jobs in Hawaii and the Virgin Islands, building houses with Habitat for Humanity in Nicaragua and Boston, serving in the Peace Corps in Bolivia and much more.

Maria Termini is the author of the book, *Silkscreening*. Her works of creative non-fiction, "Hurray Hitchhiker Fairy Godmother" and "Almost Godiva" have been published by *Newton Magazine*. Her poetry is published in Boston's street newspaper, *Spare Change*. She has produced the CD *Leafdancer*, in which she sings the soundtrack of her life with original songs, classical and folk music.

Maria Termini lives in Massachusetts writing always, painting her inspiration, singing, gardening, and walking in the forest in solitude and beauty.

Printed in the United States
77621LV00002B/1-60

9 781424 169283